BEYOND 'GENDER AND STIR'

Reflections on gender and SSR in the aftermath
of African conflicts

Edited by

Maria Eriksson Baaz and Mats Utas

The Nordic Africa Institute
2012

NAI Policy Dialogue is a series of short reports on policy relevant issues concerning Africa today. Aimed at professionals working within aid agencies, ministries of foreign affairs, NGOs and media, these reports aim to inform the public debate and to generate input in the sphere of policymaking. The writers are researchers and scholars engaged in African issues from several disciplinary points of departure. Most have an institutional connection to the Nordic Africa Institute or its research networks. The reports are internally endorsed and reviewed externally.

Indexing terms
Africa
Conflicts
Police
Armed forces
Defence policy
Gender roles
Peacekeeping
Women's participation
Security sector reform
Post-conflict reconstruction
Case studies

The opinions expressed in this volume are those of the authors and do not necessarily reflect the views of Nordiska Afrikainsitutet.

Language checking: Peter Colenbrander
Cover photo: Mats Utas
Recruitment poster from Buchanan, Liberia
ISSN 1654-6709
ISBN 978-91-7106-728-9
© The authors and Nordiska Afrikainstitutet 2012
Production: Byrå4
Print on demand, Lightning Source UK Ltd.

Innehåll

Beyoond 'Gender and Stir'

Reflections on gender and SSR in the aftermath of African conflicts

Maria Eriksson Baaz and Mats Utas

Introduction

It is widely acknowledged that security sector reform (SSR) efforts need to be gendered. However, while there is agreement on this basic point (at least in official discourse), there is less concurrence on what gendering means and how it should be achieved. In debates on these issues, one steps into hazy and contested terrain, particularly in larger forums involving both practitioners and researchers.

Being largely a policy field, gender and SSR is quite understudied and under-analysed. It is a field characterised by handbooks rather than empirical studies of how security institutions are already gendered. Moreover, it is a field dominated by manuals rather than analytical discussions of gender and the possible ramifications of various conceptualisations.

This text is not a manual. Instead, the main aim of this policy dialogue is to unpack some aspects of the gender and SSR discourse. What do we mean by gendering security sector reform? What are the main challenges to and limitations in the ways in which we presently understand and work with gender in defence and police reform? The policy dialogue is a result of a workshop on Gender and Security Sector Reform in post-conflict Societies in Africa: Challenges, Opportunities and Lessons Learned, held in Stockholm on 6–7 December 2010 and organised by the Nordic Africa Institute, Uppsala in collaboration with the Africa Programme of the Swedish National Defence College. The workshop gathered researchers, policymakers and practitioners from various institutions such as the London School of Economics, the University of Bristol, the Institute for Security Studies (South Africa), Geneva Centre for the Democratic Control of the Armed Forces (DCAF), the Mozambique Ministry of Defence, the North-South Centre (Ottawa), the Centre for Conflict Management (Rwanda), Fafo (Norway), EU, the Swedish Defence Forces, Sida and the Swedish Ministry for Foreign Affairs. Some of the contributions are published in this policy dialogue.

While one of the issues discussed during the workshop was the limitations and fluidity of the concept of SSR itself, this policy dialogue mainly addresses gender and the gendering of security institutions and does not discuss the concept of SSR in any depth.[1]

Problematising the Meaning of Gender on SSR

One of the conclusions drawn by the contributors to this policy dialogue is that the conceptions of gender underpinning present SSR interventions suffer from several limitations, which have problematical implications for the discursive practice of SSR intervention (and, it could be argued, for more general struggles for gender equality). 'Gender and SSR' tend to be translated into the representation of women in security forces and 'add women and stir' strategic interventions. As the contributors to this volume highlight, there are several problems associated with this narrow conception of gender and SSR.

One is lack of attention to and formulaic approaches to masculinities. As in many other areas, gender in SSR discourse tends to signify women. As Higate (p. 31) concludes, in military institutions, 'masculinity assumes a deeply contradictory status ... as both explicit and hidden,' as 'in/visible.' Moreover, the 'in/visible' tends to emerge as already known through the concept of militarised masculinity. Militarised masculinity is ascribed various characteristics that are assumed to be shared by military males globally (in contrast to civilian males, and both military and civilian women). This dominant imagery of a homogenised, globalised, militarised masculinity is surely incomplete. While they are shaped in a global landscape, military masculinities are constructed in national and local contexts and are also often articulated in various ways within different sections and parts of the same military institution. An example of this is provided in the text by Eriksson Baaz and Stern addressing militarised masculinities in the Congolese Army (the FARDC). This text clearly highlights the particular national and local ways in which military identities are produced and the limitations of a homogenised concept of 'military masculinity.'

Examples such as these underscore the dangers of adopting a simplified notion of militarised masculinity and point to the need for more qualitative studies analysing how security institutions are already gendered. As Higate

---

1   Some participants argued that the present concept of SSR has severe limitations, and instead promoted the concept of Security Sector Transformation. In contrast to SSR, SST places more emphasis on the need to locate security institutions within their broader political context, recognising and addressing power relations with both elected authorities and with civil communities. It also signals the need for more profound changes that address the organisational character of security institutions, including cultural make-up and human resource practices.

concludes in his contribution, there is an urgent need to generate qualitative data that illuminate how security institutions are gendered and what masculinity (and femininity) means in various military contexts – before embarking on efforts at re-gendering. Instead, gender is assumed to be known: military men emerge as depraved, as objects to be tamed and civilised through training programmes – or simply by adding women, assumed to be inherently less violent. Despite numerous studies on women combatants and soldiers that show the variety of women's experiences of war, not only as civilian victims but also as combatants engaged in acts of violence (see Coulter, Persson and Utas in this volume), we still tend to write of women in war solely as victims and as saviours whose task it is to civilise military institutions.

As Jennings concludes in her contribution, rights-based approaches that argue for women's rights to equal access to state security institutions and peacekeeping missions have been largely absent in the larger debates. Instead, the dominant argument for including women has been highly instrumental, promoting women's participation from an operational effectiveness standpoint. The need for increased women's participation is here based on women's supposedly added value and rests on certain familiar assumptions about women's 'femininity.' The inclusion of women in security forces is often described as a 'key to success' that will improve civil-military relations, diminish violence against civilians, especially against women and particularly sexual violence. As both Hendricks and Jennings point out in their contributions, there is a lack of data supporting these claims. Moreover, the 'add women and stir politics' is also problematic, since it places the responsibility on women. As Hendricks concludes in her contribution, 'Part of the slippage that has occurred in our overzealous attempt to integrate women is that we have inadvertently shifted the burden of responsibility for creating a more secure environment for particularly women on to the shoulders of women security officers' (p. 14).

At the same time, the authors in this volume also acknowledge the persuasive value of the adding-women-for-operational-purposes argument. While this argument has gained purchase because many firmly believe that it reflects reality, its popularity is also connected to its assumed effectiveness. Referring to 'women's rights' and 'gender equality' is surely much less effective when trying to convince decision- and policymakers in conservative institutions, who have plenty of arguments lined up as to why including women is not only a bad idea but indeed dangerous for the security of people and nations.[2] This

---

2   See, for example, Gutmann (2000), van Creveld (2000) and Mitchell (1989 and 1998).

makes it difficult and irresponsible to totally discard the operational effectiveness argument. However, questions remain about the possible negative consequences of this argument. What are the potential harms of the gender stereotypes it reproduces? Do the benefits outweigh its potential harm? These and other questions are addressed by some of the authors in this volume.

As was highlighted during the workshop, the answers to these questions also tend to depend on whether your primary occupation is research or policymaking. While most researchers where critical of the operational effectiveness argument, most practitioners emphasised the need for pragmatism and the strategic importance of this argument in policymaking and for practical SSR work.

Problematising the Practiceff Gender in SSR

This policy report takes us from gender roles in wars through peacekeeping and into long-term peacebuilding and capacity-building aimed at increasing structural stability. In the short texts that follow, ideas of how to proceed with this task are presented. As recently pointed out by Cordell, 'there are hundreds of resources available on the integration of women in peacekeeping; however, the implementation of such policy – especially in the murky post-conflict context – remains unclear' (Cordell 2011:39). This holds equally true of the gender work on SSR. Resources are used off the shelf: there are ample 'toolkits' and how-to manuals around. Gender and SSR work mostly take one form: workshops, training of trainers, training of trainers training trainers, etc. In Sierra Leone, for instance, NGO people in this sector typically talk about participating in 'just another talkshop.' People talk, mainly repeat what they learned in previous workshops, but much of what they learn cannot be implemented, as it is often too far removed from realities on the ground. Politico-structural postwar realities seldom lend themselves to such implementation, yet the parties often continue their game of pretend.

As, for instance, Salahub points out in her case study in this report, corruption and indiscipline remain very much the order of the day, for example, in the reformed police force in Liberia. In that country, male police officers continue to demand sexual favours of women as an alternative bribe, despite their repeated participation in code of conduct workshops and training. Also within the police of both Liberia and Southern Sudan, Salahub and co-researchers found that 'women disproportionally bear the burden of sexual harassment due to power dynamics, poor understanding of the police and fear of professional reprisals by senior male colleagues' (p. 51).

The talkshop practice of reform leads to gendered SSR being chiefly cosmetic. Police and military generally know what is right or wrong, legal or illegal, but they also know what they can get away with and what they are likely to be punished for (cf., Eriksson Baaz and Stern 2010). Without deep and wideranging reform of the legal sector, little real change will take place. The focus in much current gender work on SSR is on reform of police, military and other security sectors, but arguably there is much too little focus on the justice sector. If this sector continues to malfunction and to be clientilistic, as is the case in most African postwar countries, reform of the security sector will matter little. If money talks in courts and personal favours are the name of the game, gendered reform of the security sector is not likely to have a durable impact.

Another built-in problem in the practice of talkshop reform is the overriding import of expatriate knowledge (frequently leading locals to confuse the words 'expat' and 'expert'). Outside interveners often turn a blind eye to the structural inequalities built into the international aid system, but many Africans, especially in conflict and post-conflict areas, are acutely aware of this. Frequent references to postcolonial perceptions of 'Western' dominance among local staff and populations highlight this. Indeed, we talk a lot about local ownership – one of the buzzwords of our time – but it is all too seldom that we really try to listen. We rarely learn from the experiences of women on the ground, but instead push our pre-packed toolkits. But these are the very people who have firsthand experience of conflict and gendered experience of use and abuse and our key aim is to help them, not promote our knowledge and agendas.

There are also different cultures *within* the 'outsider' group working with gendered SSR. This is a lesson learned from our workshop, where there was an apparent divide between practitioners and academics. Researchers tend to occupy a quite comfortable position, far from the day-to-day demands and constraints of practical SSR interventions, both in terms of the difference in tasks (analysis versus implementation) and also too often spatially, by analysing and criticising from the secure and comfortable position of a desk in a research office. As reflected in the contribution by Fabrice Ramadam, practical gender and SSR work in post-conflict settings is indeed a difficult task, particularly in the Democratic Republic of Congo (DRC), where (re-)gendering is to take place in the context of never-ending military integration, continued warring and a fractured army. In addition, the re-gendering of security institutions often occurs against the backdrop of a (paradoxical) lack of interest and commitment by both intervening and receiving actors, and is often undertaken by gender advisors who are constrained by short term contracts but are nevertheless expected to deliver quick, yet sustainable and tangible results. In this situation, yet another talkshop might be the only possible option. And academic debates and criticisms of the meaning of gender and potential pitfalls of certain conceptions might seem quite remote, and indeed rather arrogant. As policymakers and practitioners argued during the workshop, there is a need for researchers to become more humble and recognise the constraints and difficulties of making policy about and working on gender and SSR in actual post-conflict circumstances. This is surely a valid point.

In the field of gendered SSR, a researcher's knowledge seldom gets across in a way that can be used by practitioners in the field. This is particularly troublesome, since we may even work in the same community at the same time, yet apparently live and talk in parallel worlds. Yet if both parties increased their efforts and better coordinated knowledge transfer, much could be gained (and this is not to say one or other party is always right). In part, this is about letting go a little of one's professional prestige and beliefs, but chiefly it is about doing more work together – joining for a more gender-just future in African postwar countries.

References

Cordell, Kristen A., 2011, 'Peacekeeping to Peace-building from a Gender Perspective: The UNMIL case,' in *Conflict Trends*, Issue 3.

Gutmann, Stephanie, 2000, *The Kinder, Gentler Military: Can America's Gender-Neutral Fighting Force Still Win Wars?* New York: Scribner.

Mitchell, Brian, 1989, *Weak Link: The Feminisation of the American Military.* Washington DC: Regnery Publishing.

Mitchell, Brian, 1998, *Women in the Military: Flirting with Disaster.* Washington DC: Regnery Publishing.

van Creveld, Martin, 2000, 'The Great Illusion: Women in the Military,' *Millennium* 29, no. 2.

Research on Gender and SSR in Africa
Challenges and Gaps
Cheryl Hendricks

Introduction

Integrating gender into security sector reform programmes in Africa has become a standard part of SSR policies and practices. Research documenting its implementation and analysing the epistemology, assumptions, processes, gains and challenges, however, remains scanty. Toolkits, guidelines, workshop reports and policy papers, as opposed to rigorous analysis, remain the dominant means of disseminating information on gender and SSR in Africa. This is in marked contrast to the general literature on SSR and governance in Africa.

In part, the paucity of research on gender and SSR can be attributed to the continued under-representation of women in this field of practice and study and the relatively recent entry of gender into SSR programming. UN Security Council Resolution 1325 (2000) drew attention to the need for a more gender-representative and responsive security sector, while UN Security Council Resolution 1820 (2008) made explicit the need to integrate gender into SSR. In 2004, the UN Department of Peacekeeping Operations best practices unit produced a gender resource package that indicated the need for women's representation in the security sector and how this could be attained. In 2009, the OECD-DAC handbook on SSR added a chapter on integrating gender awareness and equality that detailed the significance of gender equality for SSR, how to conduct a gender-responsive SSR assessment and the entry points for gender issues in SSR (OECD-DAC 2009; Mobekk 2010:282). These guidelines have been supplemented by the 'Gender and SSR Toolkit' (2008), 'Gender and SSR Training and Resource Package' (2009) and 'Examples from the Ground' (2011) produced by the Geneva Centre for the Democratic Control of the Armed Forces (DCAF).

The aim of this paper is to provide a general overview of what SSR entails, why it is important to integrate gender into SSR programming as outlined by the guidelines and toolkits, and then to tease out the major arguments presented in the research on gender and SSR in general and in Africa in particular. The paper will conclude by pointing to research challenges and gaps within the gender and SSR field.

Nature and Importance of Security Sector Reform

SSR is generally viewed as a system-wide approach that seeks to ensure democratic and civilian control of the security sector broadly defined, and the development of an effective and efficient security sector. The DCAF tool, 'Gender and Security Sector Reform Examples from the Ground,' notes that:

it is a process aimed at ensuring that security and justice providers:
- Deliver effective and efficient security and justice services that meet people's needs
- Are accountable to the state and its people
- Operate within a framework of democratic governance, without discrimination and with full respect for human rights and the rule of law. (DCAF 2011:1)

The Global Facilitation Network's 'SSR Guide for Beginners' (2007) asserts that 'SSR aims to create a secure environment that is conducive to development, poverty reduction, good governance and in particular the growth of democratic institutions based on the rule of law.'

SSR is therefore viewed as a transformative political process, theoretically grounded in the human security paradigm that links security and development. It promotes the principles of democratic oversight and accountability, rule of law, respect for human rights, legitimacy, people-centredness, local ownership, inclusion, diversity, effectiveness and efficiency of security services, all with the aim of improved delivery of security services for both the state and its citizens.

The post-conflict period, SSR practitioners contend, is the opportune time to introduce comprehensive security reform measures, for it is a period in which the state is being reconstructed. However, SSR is also simultaneously viewed as an essential component of post-conflict reconstruction, as it is deemed to assist in preventing the recurrence of violence.

Some of the countries in Africa where SSR has been implemented, with varying emphasis and success, are Angola, Burundi, Côte d' Ivoire, DRC, Liberia, Mozambique, Rwanda, Sierra Leone and South Africa. Mark Sedra points out that 'most SSR practitioners and analysts would readily admit that while the international community of practice has achieved high marks in developing and institutionalizing the SSR concept, it has received a failing grade on implementation' (Sedra 2010:17).

There are many papers outlining the general challenges in implementing SSR as a whole. Authors point to:

1. The lack of political wherewithal, institutional frameworks and long-term outlook by donors (Sedra 2010:17);
2. Lack of buy-in by recipients or narrow elite involvement in the process, thereby undermining the cardinal principle of local ownership (Sedra 2010:17);
3. Mismatch between the problems identified within the security sector and the interventions pursued (Hutton in Sedra 2010);
4. Focus on capacity-building rather than human rights (Galetti and Wodzicki in Sedra 2010);
5. Adoption of a 'cookie cutter' approach (Sedra 2010);
6. SSR remains state-centric because engaging civil society proves challenging (Sedra 2010);
7. SSR is primarily externally driven and piecemeal versus Security Sector Transformation, which argues for a comprehensive approach that requires altering the culture and character of security actors (Bryden and Olonisakin 2010).

Necessity for Integrating Gender Into SSR

Research on gender and SSR has primarily centred on justifying why gender should be integrated into SSR programmes and on providing a compass on possible ways to effect this. The OECD-DAC handbook asserts that 'the comprehensive integration of gender equality dimensions into SSR processes is *critical* to ensuring local ownership, effective delivery of justice and security services, and strengthened inclusion, oversight and accountability' (OECD-DAC 2009:1). Because men, women, boys and girls experience security differently, SSR needs to be more gender targeted and responsive in order to be effective and sustainable (Bastick 2008). Integrating gender into SSR would therefore acknowledge and respond to the different gender 'experiences, needs, priorities and roles' and it will 'ensure equal participation of men and women within security making as well as within security system institutions' (OECD-DAC 2009:2).

Additional arguments advanced for the inclusion of gender into SSR relate to adherence to international instruments; increased operational effectiveness; specific additional human resource skills and strengths; promoting non-discrimination in the workplace; and establishing more representative institutions that mirror society, prevent human rights violations and increase the relevance and sustainability of national security policies (DCAF and UN-INSTRAW 2008). Furthermore, Bastick (2008) makes the argument that 'in a democratic state women have a right to participate in the security sector institutions as an aspect of their citizenship.'

The arguments for women's inclusion are therefore both normative and utilitarian (Stanley 2008). In fact, the utilitarian argument is often more dominant, especially regarding women's participation in peacekeeping, for it is viewed as having more traction in the male-dominated security sector. Women officers are therefore assumed to use less physical force; to be better communicators and thus better at accessing information and defusing violent conflicts, earning trust and cooperation; and to be better able to perform duties such as frisking other women and responding to gender-based violence.

Experience of integrating gender into SSR over the last five years has, however, revealed certain shortcomings. Gender has often been reduced to a focus on the inclusion of women in the security sector (Bendix 2008; Hendricks and Valasek in Bryden and Olonisakin 2010). This has meant that the concentration has been on numbers rather than on transforming power relations and the culture within the security sector. Or, as Margarete Jacob (2008) indicates, there has been a concentration on 'women as actors' to the disadvantage of 'women as beneficiaries.' Then, too, few security institutions have met their targets for including women. Bendix (2008) notes the lack of focus on masculinity within security institutions and how this reflects and reinforces cultures of violence that tend to exacerbate human insecurity. Hendricks and Valasek (2010) also speak to the need to address the sexist and violent institutional culture of the security sector if an environment conducive to the participation of women and responsive to the needs of all sectors of society is to be built. They note that 'efforts to recruit women lead to a handful of junior women in a predominantly male institution. As a survival mechanism, these women will often conform to traditional gender roles rather than challenge them' (Hendricks and Valasek 2010).

The stress on the 'value-add' of women has often meant that women's inclusion is fashioned in an 'instrumentalist' way 'that treats them either as overlooked beneficiaries or as a resource of knowledge and skill which will enhance the world of the security structures' (Clarke 2008). It has also, unfortunately, led to essentialising women in a way that has reinforced gender stereotypes. Bendix (2008) highlights this aspect by noting that women are mainly seen as victims or as peacemakers. Moreover, many of the traits that women security officials are supposedly endowed with are not empirically verified, but derive from anecdotal evidence. There is a serious lack of empirical data on the actual performance of women in the security sector, including peacekeeping. Part of the slippage that has occurred in our overzealous attempt to integrate women is that we have inadvertently shifted the burden of responsibility for creating a more secure environment for particularly women on to the shoulders of women security officers, while men continue to do what they have always done.

Although integrating gender is portrayed as 'critical' and/or the 'key to the success' of SSR, it remains an afterthought in the design and implementation of SSR programmes. Eirin Mobekk (2010) points to the gap between policy and practice in this regard, and the fact that the human and financial resources for integrating gender do not match the policy prescriptions. Salahub and Nerland also make this point by indicating that gender 'remains a discrete concern, poorly integrated into broader SSR thinking' (in Sedra 2010).

Bendix's critique of gender and SSR, furthermore, asserts that the theory informing the practice of gender and SSR is liberal feminism, in terms of which women in non-Western societies are 'portrayed as voiceless victims' and 'western donors as the necessary saviors of the oppressed women in the South' (Bendix 2008:21). SSR therefore 'runs the danger of perpetuating a colonial framework of power relations' (Bendix 2008:22). This may be the case, but Bendix would be equally guilty of not attributing agency to women in the South. For just as general SSR programmes meet with resistance when applied, so, too, do women in the South not merely uncritically accept donor-driven SSR programmes. When more empirical data is produced, how women and men in the South have identified their security needs and priorities and the processes and content of their gender mainstreaming strategies will become more evident and reveal how they adapt to the specifics of their environments.

Research Challenges and Gaps

The workshop on 'Engendering Security Sector Reform,' held in Berlin in 2008 already identified gaps that future research in the field should address (Stanley 2008:6). These remain relevant. The following areas were identified:

- Intelligence services and gender;
- Traditional justice mechanisms and gender;
- Men, masculinities and SSR;
- Case studies on gender and SSR with documented outcomes, rigorous comparative analysis and explicit criteria for measuring success and failure;
- Conditions for institutional and cultural change;
- Conceptual critiques of SSR;
- The impact of intervention forces and their influence on images of masculinity and/or security;

- At the operational level, how to convert general recognition of the need to integrate a gender perspective on SSR into specific programmes and projects.

The following could be added as areas for future research:
- What are the contributions and challenges of the few women who have entered the decision-making forums in the peace and security sector?
- How many women, in which positions, are there in various security institutions in Africa? We do not have the basic data in this regard. How do they construct their tasks and how does this experience measure up to what is reflected in the literature?
- How have women in the security sector organised themselves and what effect has this had on transforming institutional cultures and in providing more responsive security? What agency have women in the security sector in Africa used to change their conditions?
- How have African SSR measures dealt with issues of sexuality?
- How do women in conflict zones protect themselves and in other spaces access security, and what are the implications for the methods by which we currently provide security?
- Document and compare country- and security sector-specific case studies on gender and SSR in Africa.
- Correctional services and border management are neglected areas in gender and SSR.

In general, integrating gender into SSR in Africa is under-researched. This belies the actual extent to which Africa, more than most continents, has actually engaged in gendered SSR, as is reflected in the contribution of women to peacekeeping missions and in the growing numbers of women in these services, as well as in the strategies and policies that have been adopted by national and regional institutions.

References

Bastick, Megan, 2008, *Integrating Gender in Post-Conflict Security Sector Reform*, DCAF Policy Paper No. 29. Geneva: DCAF.

Bastick, Megan and Kristin Valasek, 2009, *Integrating Gender into Security Sector Reform Training Resource Package*. Geneva: DCAF.

Bendix, Daniel, 2008, 'A Review of Gender in Security Sector Reform: Bringing Post-Colonial and Gender Theory into the Debate,' in Jacob, M., D. Bendix and R. Stanley (eds), *Engendering Security Sector Reform: A Workshop Report*. Workshop hosted by the Free University Berlin.

Bryden, Alan and Funmi Olonisakin, (eds), 2010, *Security Sector Transformation in Africa*, DCAF publication. Berlin: Lit Verlag Dr W. Hopf.

Clarke, Yaliwe, 2008, 'Security Sector Reform in Africa: A Lost Opportunity to Deconstruct Militarised Masculinities?' *Feminist Africa*, 10.

DCAF, 2011, 'Gender and Security Sector Reform: Examples from the Ground.' Geneva: DCAF.

Galetti, Nicholas and Michael Wodzicki, 2010, 'Securing Human Rights: Shifting the SSR Paradigm,' in Mark Sedra (ed.), *The Future of Security Sector Reform*. Waterloo, Ontario: Centre for International Governance Innovation.

Global Facilitation Network for Security Sector Reform, 2007, *A Beginners Guide to SSR*.

Hendricks, Cheryl and Kristin Valasek, 2010, 'Gender and Security Sector Transformation – From Theory to South African Practice,' in Alan Bryden and Funmi Olonisakin (eds), *Security Sector Transformation in Africa*, DCAF publication. Berlin: Lit Verlag Dr W. Hopf.

Hutton, Lauren, 2010, 'Following the Yellow Brick Road: Current and Future Challenges for SSR?,' in Mark Sedra (ed.), *The Future of Security Sector Reform*. Waterloo, Ontario: Centre for International Governance Innovation.

Margarete Jacob, 2008, 'Engendering Security Sector Reform: Sierra Leone and Liberia Compared,' in M. Jacob, D. Bendix and R. Stanley (eds), *Engendering Security Sector Reform: A Workshop Report* (p. 6). Workshop hosted by the Free University Berlin.

Mobekk, Eirin, 2010, 'Gender, Women and Security Sector Reform,' *International Peacekeeping* 17, no. 2:282.

OECD-DAC, 2009, 'Section 9: Integrating Gender Awareness and Equality,' *OECD DAC Handbook on Security System Reform*.

Salahub, Jennifer E. and Krista Nerland, 2010, 'Just add gender? Challenges to Meaningful Integration of Gender in SSR policy and Practice,' in Mark Sedra (ed.), *The Future of Security Sector Reform*. Waterloo, Ontario: Centre for International Governance Innovation.

Schulz, Sabrina and Christina Yeung, 2008, 'Private Military and Security Companies and Gender,' in Megan Bastick and Kristin Valasek (eds) *Gender and Security Sector Reform Toolkit*. Geneva: DCAF, OSCE/ODIHR, UN-INSTRAW.

Sedra, Mark (ed.), 2010, *The Future of Security Sector Reform*, Waterloo. Ontario: Centre for International Governance Innovation.

Stanley, Ruth, 2008, 'Introduction,' in M. Jacob, D. Bendix and R. Stanley (eds), *Engendering Security Sector Reform: A Workshop Report*. Workshop hosted by the Free University Berlin.

Women's Participation in UN Peace Operations
Agents of Change or Stranded Symbols?

Kathleen Jennings

Introduction

Increasing women's participation in peacemaking, peacekeeping and peace-building has been an important goal for UN peacekeeping since the passage in 2000 of UN Security Council Resolution 1325 on women, peace and security. Attempts to operationalise this goal have included the establishment or expansion of a 'gender infrastructure' in the headquarters and missions of the Department of Peacekeeping Operations (DPKO). This includes gender units, gender advisors, gender-related training and guidelines development and various gender mainstreaming efforts. There has also been an institutional push to increase the numbers of uniformed and civilian women in UN peacekeeping operations (PKOs) within the recruitment constraints by which the UN is bound.[1]

This policy brief[2] reviews the existing evidence relating to the impact of uniformed women peacekeepers – military or police – in UN peacekeeping operations. First, it lists the arguments most commonly used to advocate increased women's participation in PKOs. A thread running through these arguments is that increasing the number of women in a PKO will improve the operational effectiveness of the mission. In other words, the dominant form of argument is instrumentalist: deploying more women peacekeepers is seen as necessary to achieving a more successful mission, and not as an end in itself. There then follows a closer examination of these arguments, focusing on a) the available evidence for these claims, and b) the assumptions underlying

---

1   The UN can request, but cannot mandate, more women military peacekeepers, as the composition of the military force supplied to a peacekeeping mission is ultimately at the discretion of the troop-contributing country. The UN has somewhat more discretion over the gender balance among military observers, UN police and civilian staff.

2   An early draft of this paper was presented at the workshop on Gender and Security Sector Reform in post-Conflict Societies in Africa organised by the Nordic Africa Institute and the Swedish National Defence College (Stockholm, 6-7 December 2010). Funding for the latter paper was provided by the Norwegian Peacebuilding Centre, NOREF.

them. Here I contend that many of the claims regarding women's increased participation in PKOs are at present inflated – unsurprisingly, given the still extremely small number of uniformed women personnel in these missions – and based on 'affirmative gender essentialisms' (Helms 2003:16). Finally, there is a brief discussion of whether current attempts to increase women's participation in PKOs amounts to 'selling' gender, or selling it out. This discussion is placed in the context of a larger debate in feminist circles about the most effective ways to advance gender equality. This is a debate on both tactics and principles, and is unlikely to be resolved anytime soon.

Why More Women in Peacekeeping Operations?
The Operational Effectiveness Argument

First, a clarification is in order. Increasing women's participation in PKOs is not the same as 'mainstreaming gender' in peacekeeping. Indeed, as set out in the 1995 Beijing Conference and subsequent documents, gender mainstreaming actually has little to do with simply recruiting women into existing institutions, a policy many feminists dismiss as 'add women and stir.' Instead, gender mainstreaming is an attempt to institutionalise gendered approaches in the design and implementation of legislation and policy.[3] Conversely, Resolution 1325 specifically links increases in women's participation in peacemaking, peacekeeping and peacebuilding – and within member state peace and security institutions – to improvements in women's situations in conflict and post-conflict environments. According to Resolution 1325, appointing or recruiting more women leaders, decision-makers, military or police officers and foot soldiers is a means of better protecting the safety and rights of women and girls. Furthermore, ensuring women's participation at all levels is linked to the 'maintenance and promotion of international peace and security.'

Resolution 1325 has situated women's interests, experiences and challenges squarely within the peace and security agenda. It has been crucial in raising the visibility and importance of 'gender issues' in UN peacekeeping, and has

---

3   Specifically, gender mainstreaming refers to 'the process of assessing the implications for women and men of any planned action, including legislation, policies or programmes in all areas and at all levels. It is a strategy for making the concerns and experiences of women and men an integral dimension of design, implementation, monitoring and evaluation of policies and programmes in all political, economic and societal spheres so that women and men benefit equally and inequality is not perpetuated. The ultimate goal is to achieve gender equality'. Agreed Conclusions of the Economic and Social Council, 1997/2.

helped normalise the idea that women's equitable involvement in peace processes and, more generally, in the political and economic life of their society is vital to a sustainable peace. Nonetheless, Resolution 1325's focus on women (rather than gender), and representation and participation (rather than types of approaches), makes it susceptible to the 'add women and stir' mindset. For example, the UN has set a target of 20 per cent women police officers in UNPOL by 2014, while encouraging troop-contributing countries to include more women soldiers in their forces. These efforts notwithstanding, the number of uniformed women peacekeepers remains small, with women today constituting 3 per cent of military peacekeepers and 9 per cent of UN police.

In the grey and academic literature advocating increased women's participation in peacekeeping, a number of arguments tend to recur.[4] These overlap and reinforce one another, but some overarching themes can be identified. They include:

Protection: PKOs with more women peacekeepers are better able to protect citizens, especially women and children, because women peacekeepers bring a greater awareness of and sensitivity to their particular needs and challenges, and because women peacekeepers are less intimidating or provocative than men peacekeepers;

Sexual violence (1) – victims' assistance: Women peacekeepers ensure a more compassionate or empathetic response to victimised women and children, especially those that have been sexually assaulted. It is often claimed that it is 'easier' for a raped woman to talk to another woman about her assault;

Sexual violence (2) – deterrence: By having a 'civilising' effect on their male colleagues, women's presence ensures a better behaved, less corrupt and less abusive peacekeeping operation;

Sexual violence (3) – incidence: with regard to the problem of sexual exploitation or abuse (SEA) committed by UN personnel, women are less likely to be perpetrators, thus lowering the overall level of SEA committed;

Practical advantages: Women peacekeepers are able to search local women at checkpoints; can establish better relations with local women's groups; and can improve intelligence-gathering about the local community through better access to local women and/or a broader understanding of what constitutes a security threat;

Inspiration: Women peacekeepers contribute to more equitable gender re-

---

4   See, for example, Bertolazzi (2010); UN Department of Peacekeeping Operations (2000, 2004); UNIFEM (2007); Cordell (2009); Bridges and Horsfall (2009:120-30); Olsson and Tryggestad (eds) (2001).

lations within the local society, by serving as role models or mentors for local women and girls.

The sum of these various arguments is that the presence of women peacekeepers contributes to a more *effective* peacekeeping operation, owing to the abovementioned talents, attributes or practical advantages.

Advocates of increased women's participation may also make arguments from principle – for example, by pointing out that having more women peacekeepers contributes to the goal of a gender-equal, representative peacekeeping mission, where gender equality and representativeness are seen as ends in themselves. However, it is notable that these kinds of rights-based arguments have become increasingly marginal in the literature, rhetoric and institutional strategy relating to women peacekeepers, in favour of the instrumentalist argument stressing women's positive impact on operational effectiveness.[5] This is an instrumentalist argument insofar as the 'real goal' behind recruiting more women in uniform (presumably gender equality) is supplanted by a more palatable alternative claim (adding women makes existing institutions work better, without threatening their core functions or identity).

It is, of course, possible that the real goal is not gender equality at all, but only concerns improving the functioning and effectiveness of PKOs, militaries and police. In this case, the argument would no longer be instrumentalist, but it would not necessarily be feminist either. It seems unlikely that operational effectiveness is the only objective, given that it is gender advisors, gender units and feminists/women's groups – and not generals or police chiefs – doing most of the advocating for implementing 1325. Nevertheless, it may be the case that those most engaged in advocating 1325, especially within the UN DPKO system, are unsympathetic to distinctions between rights-based and instrumentalist arguments.[6]

Regardless, the inescapable conclusion is that an argument based on rights or principles has been deemed insufficient when it comes to uniformed personnel. Instead, the prevailing argument for women's inclusion is that a) women bring something to PKOs that men do not, and b) this contributes to more effective operations. This is evidenced by UN Secretary-General Ban

---

5 By institutional strategy, I am referring to the work of gender advisers, gender units, and gender-related training conducted by DPKO trainers or by outside groups endorsed by DPKO. This is not always a coordinated strategy, but rather a coalescing of norms, tactics, and evolving best practices. Literature and rhetoric refers to UN documents relating to gender and peacekeeping and/or Resolution 1325 and other relevant resolutions, as well as statements made by UN officials.

6 See, for example, Baumgärtner (2010). This point will be developed further below.

Ki-Moon's statement to a meeting on increasing women's participation in policing: 'Gender parity is as important here [in policing] as it is across our agenda. It is not an end in itself. It is a means to an end: greater efficiency, greater effectiveness. By empowering women within the United Nations we are not just upholding the principles for which we stand. We are making ourselves a better Organization' (UN News Center 2010).

Analysing the Argument
Part 1: Current Evidence and the Problem of Impact

So what is the evidence regarding the impact of women peacekeepers? Here some caution is warranted: at present the number of women uniformed peacekeepers is so low, and the official reform movement itself so recent, that – despite some interesting and critical work being done on the issue – unambiguous or robust evidence on the benefit of women peacekeepers is hard to come by. Much of the evidence is at this stage anecdotal and *ad hoc*. It is also to a large degree based on the assessments of women peacekeepers themselves, or of their male colleagues or commanding officers. Yet it would be disingenuous to leap to the conclusion that women's participation brings no benefits.

Indeed, there is some indication that women peacekeepers take a different approach to uniformed peacekeeping tasks than men in some of the ways featured in the arguments previously listed. Examples found in the literature – again, primarily sourced from women peacekeepers themselves – include women peacekeepers befriending and assisting local women, whether on an informal, individual basis or through more formal contacts with women's groups; women peacekeepers organising toy give-aways, school construction or clean-up and other outreach activities for local communities; and women peacekeepers helping to de-escalate tensions that had arisen between their male colleagues and locals, or providing solace to distressed local women.[7] Such efforts are generally presented as generating goodwill within the affected community or group, and/or preventing potential problems in the peacekeeper-local relationship from arising.

Conversely, there is to date little evidence bearing out the various arguments related to sexual violence (victims' assistance, deterrence or incidence). In particular, the deterrence argument – that women peacekeepers will have a

---

7   See, for example, Bridges and Horsfall (2009); Bertolazzi (2010); Cordell (2009); Barth (2004); Valenius (2007:510-23). For a conflicting view, see Sion (2008:561-85).

'civilising' effect on men peacekeepers, thus reducing the prevalence of prostitution or SEA in the mission area – is found wanting.[8] Instead, it seems that women peacekeepers adapt their own behaviour to the behaviour of the majority group, namely men. In order to be accepted by their male colleagues, they become 'one of the boys' – at least tolerating, if not encouraging, crude banter and highly sexualised behaviour. Alternatively, some women take the opposite approach by self-segregating: by abstaining from group activities where they suspect the men will be seeking out women or misbehaving but not actively doing anything to stop it.

Meanwhile, the other two aspects of the sexual violence argument (improved victims' assistance and decreased incidence) have received scant scrutiny, as has the argument that women peacekeepers serve as role models for local women. The assertion that the presence of women peacekeepers is comforting to women victims of sexual violence is extremely difficult to assess, which has not prevented it from becoming a truism. This is despite the fact that, as some researchers have described, locals are just as likely to 'see the uniform' as they are to 'see the gender'; and moreover, that women peacekeepers themselves may be no better equipped, or more willing, than their male counterparts to comfort and counsel victims of sexual violence.[9]

As noted above, it is unwise at this point to draw firm conclusions on the impact of women peacekeepers. This is especially so given that the already small percentage of women peacekeepers can be further categorised as women in a position to come into contact with locals and those whose work assignments essentially keep them confined to base or compound. In some units or battalions, all or most of the women rarely interact with anyone other than fellow peacekeepers. Yet it is worth noting that even women in jobs that take them outside the base often have very limited or superficial contact with locals.[10] This situation is not unique to women peacekeepers. Indeed, segregation between peacekeepers (especially military peacekeepers) and locals is increasingly characteristic of UN peacekeeping missions (Duffield 2010:453–

8   See, for example, Valenius (2007); Barth (2004); Sion (2008); Jennings (2008); Simic (2010:188-99).

9   On 'seeing the uniform,' see Simic (2010); Barth (2004). On women peacekeepers' potential uneasiness with local women, see Jennings (2008); (Henry forthcoming).

10 See, for example, Henry (forthcoming); Barth (2004).

74).[11] Nevertheless, it implies that even significantly increased numbers of women peacekeepers may not dramatically change the way the mission looks or feels to local residents. If peacekeepers as a group keep themselves at arm's length from locals, then the gender composition of those distant peacekeepers may not be particularly important. Furthermore, if mission policy (or battalion or unit policy) limits the opportunity for contact between peacekeepers and locals, then it is unrealistic to expect individual women peacekeepers to buck this trend. These sorts of countervailing pressures demonstrate how fraught the issue of impact can be. Even if the claims made on behalf of women peacekeepers are correct, they may not bear fruit unless the prevailing mode of doing peacekeeping changes (in which case, how will we know they are correct?). But so long as the operational effectiveness argument is dominant, the issue of evidence must be addressed. If one contends that women peacekeepers improve operational effectiveness, how is that claim verified?

Assessing the impact of issues as political and sprawling as gender and peacekeeping is a difficult, complex and controversial task. The way one approaches it depends on how the mission mandate and how 'effectiveness' are defined, and this in turn reflects the agenda, interests and institutional affiliation of those doing the defining. One way of sidestepping these debates is to set numerical targets or quotas for women's participation, where the quotas themselves serve as a proxy for impact. But as feminist critics of 'add women and stir' approaches have been arguing for decades, numerical targets don't say anything about impact. All they say is that more (or fewer) women have been deployed in peacekeeping operations, not the implications of their presence. It does not follow that simply increasing the number of women in the uniformed peacekeeping will *necessarily* increase their influence within the operation, or change the way the mission operates in relation to local citizens. These are simply assumptions, which will be unpacked in the next section.

Analysing the Argument
Part 2: The Woman Peacekeeper and 'Affirmative Essentialisms'

The question of impact relates to the peacekeeping operation or the local population, or both. That is, the subject of study is not women peacekeepers *per se*, but the effect that they have on the functioning of a mission and/

---

11 Jennings (2008) also discusses how peacekeeper training on sexual exploitation and abuse seems designed to scare peacekeepers out of casual or unmediated contact with locals.

or the welfare of local residents. However, it is also interesting to examine what the arguments in favour of women peacekeepers seem to assume about women as a group. How are women constructed by the operational effectiveness argument?[12]

Strikingly, the image that appears is far from progressive. Much of the argument hinges on the assertion, whether implicit or explicit, that it's not what women *do*, but who they *are*, that makes the difference. Or more precisely: the way women 'do' peacekeeping is inseparable from the way women peacekeepers 'are,' which is to say noticeably different from 'normal' (men) peacekeepers. Women are more compassionate and empathetic than men – thus making them better able to bond with local women, or comfort victims of sexual violence, or notice disturbances in the community that men would be oblivious to. Women are less sexually driven, or at least better able to control their sexual drive, than men, thus making them less likely to sexually exploit locals. They are also no-nonsense disciplinarians, which is why their presence shames or tames their male colleagues, keeping them from sexual misbehaviour. Women have better interpersonal skills – they connect better – than men, thus enabling them to be mentors to other women, and also to defuse situations that men ignite. Women are simply less threatening than men, even when highly trained, wearing a uniform, and carrying a weapon. Indeed, this lack of overt menace makes them model peacekeepers (DeGroot 2001). Cumulatively, the traits that seem to underpin the ideal-type woman peacekeeper – compassion, empathy, asexualised, disciplined and disciplining, connector, consensus-seeker – are also often associated with that most typical of womanly acts, mothering.

That these claims reinforce some traditional stereotypes of women does not mean they are necessarily misguided or harmful. In the context of the operational effectiveness argument, they are employed in order to assert a positive message about women's capabilities and resourcefulness. Some women peacekeepers themselves point to these qualities when discussing what they bring to their job, often (perhaps paradoxically) at the same time emphasising their professionalism and training.[13] Helms refers to these types of tropes as 'affirmative gender essentialisms' (Helms 2003:16). This captures the fact that, while the constitutive qualities may be generally positive, they nonetheless

---

12 Here I focus on the operational effectiveness argument since it is the most prevalent, and since the arguments used to construct it are the most loaded with assumptions.

13 See, for example, Henry (forthcoming); Barth (2004).

dismiss women's diverse capabilities, experiences and interests in favour of a particular ideal based on the 'essential' character of womanhood. That these essentialisms are flattering does not make them less patronising or otherwise unproblematic. For example, the affirmative essentialist ideal overlooks the possibility that women are attracted to careers in the military or police for the same pragmatic reasons as many men – for a stable job, a relatively decent salary, the opportunity to challenge themselves, etc. – and, by extension, are interested in participating in peacekeeping operations not primarily to help other women, but rather to improve their own career prospects or increase their earning potential. Indeed, it may be that ambitious women would spe-cifically prefer not to work on 'women's issues' in PKOs, for fear of being ghettoised and barred from what are perceived as more prestigious positions. Moreover, and perhaps especially in the military, it is often the case that the women soldiers and officers are the *least* convinced of their ability to enact change beyond their immediate work environment, and sometimes not even there.[14] This is likely a realistic response for women working in institutions that remain not just male-dominated, but extremely masculine in orientation, ideology and functioning.

Yet such a response from women 'inside the system' illustrates how large a burden of responsibility the operational effectiveness argument puts on the shoulders of women peacekeepers, who by their very presence are supposed to make the mission better. There are two related issues here. One is the fea-sibility of genuine change occurring when there are still so few women in the otherwise male-dominated peacekeeping apparatus. In particular, why should we expect that, in the case of women soldiers, the system will adapt to them rather than that they will adapt to the system? Are women expected to be uniquely resistant to the dominant masculinities ingrained in military (or pea-cekeeping) service? From an operational effectiveness perspective, the answer seems to be yes, since much of the argument is built on affirmative gender essentialisms that (it must be assumed) are unaffected by training and deploy-ment. But this is a dubious proposition.[15] Indeed, the opposite reaction seems more plausible: that woman recruits will 'estrange themselves from "femini-nity" as it is portrayed by the army and mock other women who are viewed as stereotypical females' (Sion 2008:580). Such strategies will likely continue

---

14 See, for example, DeGroot (2001). WIIS (2010) makes a similar case for women in high-level peace and security careers in the US State Department.
15 For more on masculinities and military training with specific reference to pea-cekeeping, see Whitworth (2004:ch. 6).

unless the institution itself is 're-gendered.'[16] Thus, rather than being agents of change, they may end up being stranded symbols.

The second issue is the unfairness of designating women as the only change agents – that is, putting the onus of responsibility on women (some of whom have little desire to 'fly the flag' for their fellow women), rather than on the men who still dominate and largely populate the institution of UN uniformed peacekeeping. Shifting the burden of change on to women lets men off the hook, making even more unlikely the kind of transformational change mentioned above. If compassion, empathy and sensitivity to the local population are important to the functioning of the PKO, then why can't men also be compassionate, empathetic and sensitive?

A final point worth mentioning relates specifically to the assumption that women peacekeepers will have a better relationship with the local population, perhaps even serving as mentors to other women and girls. This expectation exists despite the formidable linguistic and cultural differences that tend to exist between the peacekeepers and locals – differences which one could expect to impact peacekeepers' ability to communicate with and understand the specific needs of local women. Cynically, one could say that there seems to be the expectation that the simple act of being a woman will transcend the economic, cultural, linguistic and possibly religious, racial or ethnic differences, fostering open communication based on a kind of shared global sisterhood.[17]

Selling Gender, or Selling Out?

The above criticisms of the operational effectiveness argument – that it instrumentalises gender equality, depends on evidence of impact that may be difficult to establish and is based on affirmative gender essentialisms – have provoked wariness in some feminists.[18] Their concern is that an argument for women's participation that depends on common stereotypes of women, while avoiding serious interrogation of the prevailing gender regimes (i.e., dominant masculinities) within uniformed peacekeeping, is self-defeating. Getting more women into UN peacekeeping is a hollow victory if it means that those women are expected to conform to traditionally 'feminine' roles or modes of behaviour. Indeed, such a situation may only serve to reinforce conserva-

---

16 On 'regendered armies,' see Cockburn and Hubic (2002:103-21).

17 See especially Henry (forthcoming) on this point, and Aagenæs (2010).

18 See Aagenæs (2010) for a particularly critical account; also Valenius (2007); Sion (2008).

tive gender regimes based on strictly demarcated divisions between the sexes, rather than to break them down. Conversely, placing too-high expectations on women peacekeepers could lead to disillusionment or backlash if those expectations are unable to be fulfilled. Thus, 'selling' gender – without taking onboard the larger political project of gender equality – risks selling it out.

Advocates of the operational effectiveness argument tend to find these critiques overblown, exasperating and counterproductive.[19] They argue that establishing access for women is the most important task, and that once a sufficient level of participation is obtained, the evidence of women's effectiveness will be both clear and irrefutable. Thus, any argument that convinces the right people to give women a chance is the best one to use. In conservative institutions such as militaries, the most persuasive argument is the one that shows very clearly how the proposed change will improve the status quo. This is not achieved through political and potentially polarising advocacy of women's rights or equality, but through examples that the listener can relate to. There is no contradiction in 'selling' women's participation one way to one audience, and another way to another audience. The point is to make the sale. Concerns about reinforcing stereotypes or consolidating existing gender regimes are seen more as an excuse for inaction than anything to be taken seriously. If the alternative is to carry on with negligible levels of women's participation, then worrying about the potential negative consequences of the operational effectiveness argument seems to be misplacing priorities.

This debate over tactics and principles has played out recurrently throughout the feminist movement, and is unlikely ever to be fully resolved. So long as the debate is constructive rather than personalised or dismissive, both sides have an important role to play in setting realistic expectations and identifying barriers to progress for women peacekeepers.

Conclusion

Increasing women's participation in peacekeeping operations has the potential to benefit all parties: the local residents of the mission area, the peacekeeping operation and individual peacekeepers, both women and men. Including a more diverse range of experiences, capabilities and viewpoints at all levels of a PKO opens up the possibility of missions that are more responsive, less clubby and not as prone to group-think. Yet it is important to remember that

---

19 This observation is based on personal discussions with several people involved in advocating increased women's participation in UN peacekeeping.

gender is not the only relevant axis of identity. Class, race, religion, education, language, ethnicity, nationality, North/South – all feature heavily in the intersection of peacekeepers and locals. The host society is itself also striated along these lines, and in some key ways local elites may have more in common with peacekeepers than with their own fellow citizens.

The point of this observation is to show that the encounter between peacekeepers and locals can be fraught in many ways. The presence of women peacekeepers can sometimes make this encounter run smoother than it otherwise might. In other cases, the gender of the peacekeeper is secondary to the barriers posed by language, class, education or the simple fact that the peacekeeper is uniformed and (possibly) armed. This complexity shows the limitations of essentialist arguments about what women peacekeepers can achieve. At the same time, sceptics of such essentialist arguments must be careful to ensure that, in criticising the arguments made for women peacekeepers, they are not giving ammunition to anti-feminists.

References

Aagenæs, V., 2010, 'Who Needs Who?: A Critical Analysis of the Debate on Women in UN Peacekeeping Operations,' MA thesis submitted to the School of Oriental and African Studies, University of London.

Barth, E.F., 2004, 'The United Nations Mission in Eritrea/ Ethiopia – Gender(ed.) Effects' in Olsson, L., I. Skjelsbæk, E.F. Barth and K. Hostens (eds), *Gender Aspects of Conflict Interventions: Intended and Unintended Consequence.* Oslo: Prio.

Baumgärtner,U., 2010, 'Learning to Speak a "Masculine" Language: Rationalisation of Gender Equality in the United Nations Peacekeeping Bureaucracy,' paper presented at the International Studies Association Annual Conference, New Orleans.

Bertolazzi, F., 2010, *Women with a Blue Helmet: The Integration of Women and Gender Issues in UN Peacekeeping Missions.* Dominican Republic: UN-INSTRAW Working Paper Series.

Bridges, D. and D. Horsfall, 2009, 'Increasing Operational Effectiveness in UN Peacekeeping: Toward a Gender-Balanced Force,' *Armed Forces and Society* 36, no. 1:120–30.

Cockburn, C. and M. Hubic, 'Gender and the peacekeeping military: A view from Bosnian women's organizations,' in Cockburn, C. and D. Zarkov (eds), *The Postwar Moment: Militaries, Masculinities and International Peacekeeping.* London: Lawrence and Wishart.

Cordell, K., 2009, 'Gender-Related Best Practices in Peacekeeping Operations in Liberia: 2003–2009, mimeo.

DeGroot, G., 2001, 'Few Good Women: Gender Stereotypes, the Military and Peacekeeping,' in Olsson, L. and T.L. Tryggestad (eds), *Women and International Peacekeeping*. London: Frank Cass.

Duffield, M., 2010, 'Risk-Management and the Fortified Aid Compound: Everyday Life in Post-Interventionary Society,' *Journal of Intervention and Statebuilding* 4, no. 4:453–74.

Helms, E., 2003, 'Women as agents of ethnic reconciliation? Women's NGOs and International Intervention in Postwar Bosnia-Herzegovina,' *Women's Studies International Forum* 26, no. 1:16.

Jennings, K.M., 2008, *Protecting Whom: Approaches to sexual exploitation and abuse in UN peacekeeping operations*. Oslo: Fafo.

Jennings, M. Henry, 2008, 'Peacexploitation? Interrogating Labor Hierarchies and Global Sisterhood amongst Indian and Uruguayan Female Peacekeepers,' *Globalisations*, forthcoming.

Olsson, L. and T.L. Tryggestad, 2001, 'Introduction' in Olsson, L. and T.L. Tryggestad (eds), *Women and International Peacekeeping*. London: Frank Cass.

Simic, O., 2010, 'Does the Presence of Women Really Matter? Towards Combating Male Sexual Violence in Peacekeeping Operations,' *International Peacekeeping*, vol. 17, no. 2, 188–199.

Sion, L., 2008, 'Peacekeeping and the Gender Regime: Dutch Female Peacekeepers in Bosnia and Kosovo,' *Journal of Contemporary Ethnography* 37, no. 5:561–85.

UN Department of Peacekeeping Operations, 2000, *Mainstreaming a Gender Perspective in Multidimensional Peace Operations*, New York.

UN Department of Peacekeeping Operations, 2004, *Gender Resource Package for Peacekeeping Operations*, New York.

United Nations Development Fund for Women (UNIFEM), 2007, *Gender-Sensitive Police Reform in Post-Conflict Societies*, UNIFEM.

UN Economic and Social Council (ECOSOC), 1997, *UN Economic and Social Council Resolution 1997/2: Agreed Conclusions*, available at http://www.unhcr.org/refworld/docid/4652c9fc2.html

Ki- Moon, Ban (Secretary-General), 2010, 'Gender Parity Leads to Greater Efficiency and Effectiveness: Secretary-General tells meeting on increasing women's participation in United Nations policing,' UN News Center, New York, 4 June, available athttp://www.un.org/News/Press/docs/2010/sgsm12935.doc.htm

Valenius, J., 2007, 'A Few Kind Women: Gender Essentialism and Nordic Peacekeeping Operations,' *International Peacekeeping*14, no. 4:510–23.

Whitworth, S., 2004, *Men, Militarism and UN Peacekeeping: A Gendered Analysis*. Boulder CO: Lynne Rienner, Ch. 6.

Women in International Security (WIIS), 2010, *Progress Report on Women in Peace & SecurityCareers: US. Executive Branch*. Washington DC: WIIS.

Foregrounding the In/Visibility of Military and Militarised Masculinities

Paul Higate

Introduction

Despite at least three decades of academic debate on masculinity, policy recommendation and policy implementation, it is almost inconceivable that for many the word gender remains synonymous with 'woman.' This situation is amplified when one looks at the exemplary military or militarised setting where masculinity assumes a deeply contradictory status as both explicit and hidden: as such, we can say it is invisible.

The following discussion examines the concepts of masculinities, military masculinities and militarised masculinities before going on to look at gaps in the masculinities literature, and finally the practical challenges of bringing about positive change in pre-existing gender regimes of relevance to the SSR imperative.

Masculinity as a Concept

Within the social science canon, scholars have illuminated the hidden, naturalised power-practices of a diverse cluster of relational values, beliefs, performances and ideologies known collectively as 'masculinity' (Connell 1987, 1995, 2005; Brittan 1989; Morgan 1992; Cornwall and Lindisfarne 1994; Seidler 1997; Hearn 1998; Enloe 2000; Hopper 2000; Whitehead and Barrett 2002; Cleaver 2002; Pease and Pringle 2002; Cockburn and Zarkov 2002; Messerschmidt 2004; Parpart and Zalewski 2008). Hegemonic masculinity connotes a privileged and privileging gender identity that shapes individual and institutional possibilities according to its temporal, situational and cultural manifestations. More broadly, while masculinity is extremely difficult to define (Plummer 1999), in the final analysis its key feature is that it is *not femininity* (Hutchings 2008:389–404). However, masculinity is not a thing, a noun that names, but rather invokes configurations of contingent, sometimes contradictory, diverse social practices constituting particular gender identities, gender orders and gender regimes (Connell 2008:277–95). Biology is not destiny, and in using the word gender we invoke the particular roles and relationships, personality traits, attitudes, behaviours and values that society

31

ascribes to men and women (Valasek, Johannsen and Bastick 2009:15). Yet the word masculinity does not move easily across diverse cultural contexts. Effecting change in gender relations, gender regimes and gender orders may then require engaging innovatively and creatively with the pre-existing grain of the diverse gendered terrains of those individuals and communities whose transformation we seek.

Military Masculinity

The institution of the military is one of the most powerful arenas of social power and violence and involves (dis)embodiment, blood, guts, death, injury and psychological trauma. Armies and militia are overwhelmingly constituted by men, young men and boys. Women, young women and girls may fight alongside and/or support their male peers, though in very small numbers, and women play a key role in 'keeping the home fires burning' (Enloe 2000). In terms of death and injury, there are numerous contexts other than that of the military within which violence occurs. Military personnel are socialised in different ways (with various degrees of success) to elicit so-called 'controlled violence' under particular circumstances. However, as Connell (1995) notes:

> The relationship of masculinity to violence is more complex than appears at first sight. Institutional violence (e.g. by armies) requires more than one kind of masculinity. The gender practice of the general is different from the practice of the front-line soldier, and armies acknowledge this by training them separately (Connell 1995).

Military masculinity has been described in terms invoking a wide range of behaviours including aggressive, rational, courageous, cool, calculating, chivalrous, protective and emotionally expressive (Morgan 1994:391–2). In a wider sense, masculinity – with an unspoken allusion to military masculinity – has been accorded a diversity of influences from the 'causal' variable in war, through to an ideological construct designed to 'get men to fight' (Goldstein 2001:391). It is important to register, however, that soldiers are neither 'blindly obedient' nor subjectively homogenous. Understandings of these kinds remove agency from heterogeneous groups of individuals who may resist, mutiny, question, desert and conscientiously object as well as conform and obey. Despite the complexity here, overall the institution and its people exercise huge potential for destruction, as noted in the devastating use of force against the citizens of Fallujah in 2005 that left many hundreds of unarmed civilians dead and injured, or the Israeli Defence Force's attack on Gaza in 2009 that resulted in the deaths of over 1,000 Palestinians and 13 Israelis.

Discussion now turns to Cynthia Enloe's concept of militarism, an analytical template worthy of critique and development in regard to conceptions of military masculinities. She writes:

> Militarism is an [ideological] ... package of ideas. It is a compilation of assumptions, values and beliefs. When any person – or institution or community – embraces militarism it [he/she] is thus embracing particular value assertions about what is good, right, proper and about what is bad, wrong and improper. By embracing the ideology of militarism ... a person is also accepting [beliefs] ... about what makes human nature tick. (Enloe 2002:23)

Ideologies are grounded in power relations that constitute the conditions of possibility with which to understand one's social world, its constraints, its freedoms and one's material practice. This is another way of (re)stating the feminist maxim that, indeed, the personal is the political. In order to have influence, militarism has necessarily to function as an internally coherent, self-referential and multidimensional constellation of ideas that engender ways of seeing and structures of feeling, as the literary theorist Raymond Williams might put it. Taken in isolation, one-dimensional strands of militarist thought (for example, the belief that there can be a military 'solution' in Afghanistan), can only succeed if they chime with a wider audience – for example, the public whose shared belief (or otherwise) makes the occupation possible.

What of the human actor and her agency? Here it is important to interrogate the words 'embrace' and 'embracing' by posing the following question: how far do actors 'embrace' militarism? In preference to this framing, I would argue for the existence of a continuum of beliefs and attitudes towards militarist values – even among those who become soldiers. In the UK and US context, the armed forces are typically referred to as an 'all volunteer force' and it might easily be assumed that those enlisting 'embrace,' or at least 'accept,' the values of the organisation in which they seek membership. Notions of 'volunteering' or 'voluntarism' resonate with cluster concepts such as 'choice' and 'freedom,' and in turn invoke an unfettered agency enacted by the sovereign individual of liberal democracy. Yet, a significant proportion of those joining (predominantly) the army, do so for a combination of both push and pull factors. These could be linked on the one hand to educational incentives, through on the other to escaping poverty. In other (conflict/post-conflict) contexts there may be even less opportunity to exercise one's 'choice' to enlist. Here, coercion might be used in ways not dissimilar to the 'impressment' tactics deployed in the 17th century in the UK by 'press-gangs' who abducted men between the age of 18 and 45 and forced them to join the Royal

Navy. At the far extreme, younger men, boys and girls may have members of their family murdered, leaving them in a state of both severe trauma and extreme anomie, where joining a militia is their only hope of survival within the context of a 'surrogate family.'

The first of seven militaristic core beliefs identified by Enloe is that 'the armed force is the ultimate resolver of tensions' (Enloe 2002:23). Even here there may be some complexities, as noted in the hesitation to go to war expressed by senior British military commanders in the build-up to the invasion of Iraq in 2003. The second value, 'that human nature is prone to conflict' (Enloe 2002:23), invokes Hobbesian rather than Lockean understandings of agency as a key element of militarist thought. If it is indeed the case that human nature is prone to conflict, then why the concerted, intensive and hugely expensive time, effort and resources dedicated to training civilians to become soldiers? Surely it might be more accurate to suggest that human nature is – on the contrary – *resistant* to conflict. Third, how might a militarised masculinity respond to the notion that 'having an enemy is a natural condition'? (Enloe 2002:23). The dichotomous framing of enemy/friend is perhaps less likely to provoke debate, though even here it is worth mentioning that those perceiving themselves as civilians – or at least individuals who perceive themselves to be some distance from militaristic thought – may also regard enemies as inevitable. Is 'having an enemy a distinctive militarist trait'? Fourth is the question of hierarchies – structures that 'produce effective action' (Enloe 2002:23) and central to military organisations. Few either within or outside the military would disagree with the necessity of hierarchising social relations in this unique sphere. But once again, how far are they unique to the organisation? Fifth, what of the militaristic core belief 'that a state without a military is naïve, scarcely modern and barely legitimate'? This belief invokes the example of Costa Rica, a nation that abolished its military in 1948. Of course this is a highly unusual case, yet it does provide food for thought in respect of both what this means for the country's security and the assumption that Costa Rica will necessarily be perceived as naïve – even by those militaristic onlookers. Sixth, Enloe notes that 'in times of crisis those who are feminine need armed protection' (Enloe 2002:22). For some commentators, gender-based violence perpetrated against women, men, boys and girls exemplifies the kinds of aggressive masculinities to be found in the militarised setting and Enloe's point here is helpful in drawing out the contradictions of militarisation. Lastly, there is the observation that 'in times of crisis any man who refuses to engage in armed violent action is jeopardising his own status as a manly man' (Enloe 2002:23–4). The virulent attacks on those considered 'deserters' and 'cowards'

– most graphically illustrated by the not insignificant number of US citizens who fled to Canada in order to avoid fighting in Iraq – affirms the importance of this core belief.

Empirical Deficits – Masculinities, Law Enforcement and the Police

It is striking to note that interventions intended to effect SSR often proceed in the absence of an in-depth understanding of the agents of (potential) change to which they are addressed. To put this differently, if SSR is to facilitate a military and police sector sensitive to gendered issues among civilian men and women in the wider populace, it must proceed on an evidence base that takes account of the kinds of masculinities and femininities that constitute security sector gender orders themselves. The limited understanding of gendered police culture is not restricted to non-Western contexts, with the literature focusing on this area in the US and the UK remaining limited and dealing with such concerns as masculinity (Prokos and Pradavic 2002:439–59) and lesbian and gay police officers (Miller, Forest and Jurik 2003:355–85), for example. Seen more broadly, the critical men's studies literature remains dominated by work focusing on gendered relations in the developed countries, particularly the US and Northern Europe. While there is a small and growing literature examining 'Islamic masculinities,' 'Latin American masculinities' and 'African masculinities' (Ouzgane 2006), its utility is limited in respect of those involved in SSR. There exists a clear and pressing need to generate qualitative data that illuminates the gendered and religious sub-cultures of, for example, institutions tasked with providing security for vulnerable populations – particularly those emerging from conflict. In anecdotal terms, I have sat through numerous 'gender training' sessions conducted by well-intentioned and highly qualified trainers aimed at members of national police forces and militaries to audiences of attentive yet clearly confused students. While aspects of this critique are recognised, as noted in the acknowledgement of 'cultural issues in the DCAF 'Gender and Security Sector Training Resource Package,' there exists a paucity of understanding about exactly how gender regimes in non-Western law enforcement contexts play themselves out, and in turn shape the ways in which indigenous members of these organisations are likely to negotiate interventions managed by (mainly male) cultural outsiders. Here, an important line of inquiry would be to further investigate the intra-masculine relations between Western instructors and their local students. Little or nothing is known about how the crucial dimension of solidarity and camaraderie is developed and maintained in the Afghan or Iraqi police/military setting, where allegiances may assume a wholly different character to those noted in the UK or US, for example. Indeed, it would be worth tapping into the tacit knowledge held by former and currently serving police officers and members of militaries tasked with training security forces in respect of how they perceive the gender regimes that confront them in the classroom, on the firing range and as enacted by their students out in the community. In a less explicitly gendered sense, SSR should not be approached as a 'one-size-fits-all' project, and it would be well worth those involved in the training process to take a closer look at the historical, cultural and gendered aspects of the institutions and the people they are seeking to develop.

Conclusion

In this working paper, I have focused on the concepts of military and militarised masculinities. While not dealing explicitly with SSR in the African context, my approach has been to identify the broader complexities within these concepts, the likes of which leave more room than might typically be thought for productive engagement and reform. I have also noted that there exists a significant knowledge gap in awareness of gender, racial and religious identity regimes/orders in regard to the institutions that are the intended targets of reform. The effectiveness of reform should be evidence-led, and until a body of in-depth work has been developed regarding concerns of intra-masculine gender orders (for example), interventions may well fail to engage the very stakeholders on whom they depend for effective change.

References

Bastick, Megan and Kristin Valasek, 2009, *Integrating Gender into Security Sector Reform Training Resource Package*. Geneva: Centre for the Democratic Control of the Armed Forces.

Bastick, M., K. Valasek and A.M. Johannsen, 2009, *Gender and Security Sector Reform Training Resource Package*. Geneva: Centre for the Democratic Control of the Armed Forces, p.15.

Brittan, A., 1989, *Masculinity and Power*. Oxford: Blackwell.

Cleaver, F. (ed.), 2002, *Masculinities Matter! Men, Gender and Development*. London: Zed Press.

Cockburn, C. and D. Zarkov (ed.), 2002, *The Post-War Moment: Militaries, Masculinities and International Peacekeeping*. London: Lawrence and Wishart.

Connell, R., 1987, *Gender and Power*. Palo Alto: Stanford University Press.

Connell, R., 1995, *Masculinities*. Cambridge: Polity Press.

Connell, R., 2005, 'Globalisation, Imperialism, and Masculinities,' in M. Kimmel, J. Hearn and R. Connell. (eds), *Handbook of Studies on Men and Masculinities*. London: Sage.

Cornwall, A. and N. Lindisfarne (eds), 1994, *Dislocating Masculinity: Comparative Ethnographies*. London: Routledge.

Enloe, C., 2000, *Maneuvers*. California: University of California Press.

Enloe, C., 2002, 'Demilitarisation or more of the same? Feminist questions to ask in the post-war moment,' in Cockburn, C. and D. Zarkov (eds), *The Post War Moment*. London: Lawrence and Wishart, pp. 22–4.

Goldstein, J., 2001, *War and Gender*. Cambridge: Cambridge University Press.

Hearn, J., 1998, 'Troubled masculinities in social policy discourses,' in J. Popay, J. Hearn and J. Edwards (eds), *Men, Gender Divisions and Welfare*. London: Routledge.

Hopper, C., 2000, *Manly States: Masculinities, International Relations and Gender Politics*. Columbia: Columbia University Press.

Hutchings, K., 2008, 'Making Sense of Masculinity and War,' *Men and Masculinities* 10, no. 4:89–404.

Messerschmidt, J.W., 2004, *Flesh and Blood. Adolescent Gender Diversity and Violence*. Maryland: Rowman and Littlefield.

Miller, S. L., K.B. Forest and N.C. Jurik, 2003, 'Diversity in Blue: Lesbian and gay police officers in a masculine occupation,' *Men and Masculinities* 5, no. 4:355–85.

Morgan, D., 1994, 'Theater of War: Combat, the Military and Masculinities,' in H. Brod and M. Kaufman (eds), *Theorising Masculinities*. London: Sage.

Morgan, D., 1992, *Discovering Men*. London: Routledge.

Ouzgane, L. (ed.), 2006, *Islamic Masculinities*. London: Zed Press.

Parpart, J. and M. Zalewski, 2008, *Rethinking the Man Question: Sex, Gender and Violence in International Relations*. London: Macmillan.

Pease, B. and K. Pringle (eds), 2002, *A Man's World? Changing Men's Practices in a Globalised World*. London: Zed Press.

Plummer, K., 1999, *One of The Boys: Masculinity, Homophobia and the Modern Manhood*. New York: Harrington Park Press.

Prokos, A. and I. Pradavic, 2002, 'There Oughtta Be A Law Against Bitches: Masculinity Lessons in Police Academy Training,' *Gender, Work and Organisation* 9, no. 4:439–59.

Schrock, D. and M. Schwalbe, 2008, 'Men, Masculinity and Manhood Acts,' *Annual Review of Sociology* 35:277–95.

Seidler, V., 1997, *Man Enough: Embodying Masculinity*. London: Sage.

Whitehead, S. and F.J. Barrett (eds), 2001, *The Masculinities Reader*. Cambridge: Polity Press.

Beyond Militarised Masculinity

The case of the Democratic Republic of Congo[*]

Maria Eriksson Baaz and Maria Stern

> Our superiors say that they are fair – that it is equality. But they are not. They give the women all the good jobs. They are the ones who get training. They are the ones who get jobs as secretaries, who get to learn typing. If you look at the administrative jobs – it is only women! It is not fair. (Male corporal, 23 years)[1]

These words were spoken by a corporal in the infantry in the armed forces of the DRC. His account of the desired positions in the army (a preference echoed by many of his colleagues) contrasts quite markedly from dominant assumptions about militarised masculinity. Rather than celebrating tough, macho fighters on the frontlines or specialised units, he identified the secretary, the military clerk (in many other military contexts configured as an inferior form of masculinity, see Higate 2003) as the desired and celebrated military position.

As discussed in the introduction and in Higate's text above, militarised masculinity is often afforded various attributes that are assumed to be shared by military males globally. It is this militarised masculinity, assumed to be 'already known,' which tends to emerge as the 'object for reform' in gender and SSR interventions. This has been the case also in the DRC, where a range of external actors are involved in efforts to reform the Congolese armed forces. In the DRC, attempts to tame and reform (violent) militarised masculinity have been intimately linked to the fight against sexual violence. Consequently, the objective of gender-sensitive defence reform has been to educate Congolese soldiers about the difference between 'good' and legal and 'bad' and illegal (masculine) behaviour and to create soldiers who know about, understand and respect human rights – especially women's rights (and, in particular, women's rights to not be raped by them). As in many other post-conflict contexts (see the introduction), these efforts have largely taken the form of workshops and training sessions on human rights and international humanitarian law.

This short paper is based on our research on gender within the armed

---

[*]   This text is based on research results that have appeared elsewhere. See Eriksson Baaz and Stern (2008, 2009, 2010 and 2011).

[1]   This citation also appeared in Eriksson Baaz and Stern (2008).

forces of the DRC, conducted between 2006 and 2010 (and funded by Sida),[2] and its aim is to highlight some aspects of military masculinities as they were articulated in our interview material. By drawing attention to the manner in which the Congolese armed forces are 'already gendered' in ways that were both similar to and different from dominant presuppositions about militarised masculinity (emerging mostly from research on Western armed forces), we demonstrate the limitations of a homogenised and universalising concept of 'military masculinity.' Moreover, based on our research, we highlight some weaknesses of and challenges within gendered SSR interventions in the DRC. To what extent are current interventions attuned to the ways in which the Congolese armed forces are 'already gendered'?

Similar, yet different: militarised masculinities as shaped in global and local contexts

The soldiers and officers to whom we spoke clearly located and negotiated their military gendered identities by referring to a global military ethos and by comparing themselves to other armed forces wordwide (see Eriksson Baaz and Stern 2008, 2011). Certainly, their notions of what it means to be a good military male in the DRC bear many resemblances to the dominant and generalised notion of military masculinity. This was particularly evident in discussions about women's roles in the army. In negotiating their identities as military males in relation to women's potentially increasing participation in the armed forces, their voices often echoed traditionalist military discourses and identities articulated elsewhere. For instance, when arguing against women's inclusion in the armed forces, many soldiers referred to the classic military traditionalist argument (cf., Gutmann 2000; Mitchell 1998 and 1989; van Creveld 2000) of women's supposed physical and psychological weakness. This weakness, they explained, rendered women unsuitable for combat. Masculinity was portrayed as embodying physical strength, willingness to endure extreme physical danger and readiness to take lives, while women were cast as less aggressive, less daring and less able to cope with minor personal hurts, hence just not up to the job of combat.[3]

Moreover, as in other military settings (cf., Gutmann 2000; Mitchell 1989; van Creveld 2000), many soldiers and officers argued that having ser-

---

2   See Eriksson Baaz and Stern (2009, 2010, 2011) for more details on the approach and methodology of this research project.

3   According to this line of reasoning, including women in the armed forces will, arguably, necessarily manifest itself in a weakening of the armed forces.

ving women in the armed forces erodes unit cohesion through fraternisation and sexual distraction. They explained that instead of bonding with colleagues and engaging with the enemy, male soldiers compete with each other for the attention of women (Eriksson Baaz and Stern 2011). This argument draws on a familiar narrative, which sexualises women engaged in violence: the 'whore narrative,' which has discomfited women in the armed forces globally (cf., Sjoberg and Gentry 2007)

However, while the gendered identities articulated by the soldiers in the interviews in many ways echoed attributes associated with the generalised notion of militarised masculinity, they were also different. Our reading of soldiers' narratives highlights the ways in which the production of military identities is also locally specific. The soldiers did not simply repeat arguments and gender identities articulated elsewhere. For example, the notion of 'heroic masculine violent achievement' central to many other militarised narratives (cf., Higate in this volume and Higate 2003) was largely absent in soldiers' narratives and was expressed almost exclusively in the context of women's participation in the armed forces. Otherwise, the interview texts were characterised by a general absence of celebration of, or aspiration to, heroic violent achievement. There were few references to iconic idolised soldiers or officers who sacrificed themselves and/or performed heroically on the front lines. Instead (as the quote at the beginning of this text reveals) the soldiers overwhelmingly spoke of administration – working behind a desk – as the ultimate desirable position. For them, the ideal soldier was intimately tied to the ideal notion of masculine 'provider,' and celebrated manhood was symbolised by the affluent, urban man working in an office, with a nice house and a car, surrounded by many women. The Rambo type in the bush seemed to hold little appeal, judging from its absence in their narratives (Eriksson Baaz and Stern 2008)

Neither was the ideal soldier configured as a rapist. Rape or raping was neither linked to successful masculinity, nor presented as morally right or honourable (Eriksson Baaz and Stern 2009 and 2010). The soldiers distinguished between various types of rape (Eriksson Baaz and Stern 2009), the most common, according to them, being 'lust rape,' which they explained as a manifestation of the male sexual urge and poverty. According to this line of reasoning, it as 'somewhat unavoidable' that a man who is 'denied sex' in any way through lack of financial or other means will eventually rape. This reasoning is a familiar echo of myths about male heterosexuality, masculinity, soldiering and violence reproduced in many military contexts (cf. Enloe 2000; Wood 2009; Higate and Hopton 2003; Higate 2004; Whitworth 2007). Masculinity is here tightly linked to virility and sexual potency, and the male soldier's libido is understood as a formidable natural force, which ultimately demands sexual satisfaction from women.

Yet, while virility and maintaining multiple sexual relations was celebrated and indeed presented as a way to perform and live up to the ideals of masculinity, the soldiers never spoke of rape in this way. While they may have explained or even excused rape, they never celebrated it. In referring to instances of rape, almost all of their accounts included a statement that rape is bad and forbidden, both in military and civilian life. Some of the soldiers' stories of rapes featured a cautionary lesson or warning, thus conveying the immorality of rape (Eriksson Baaz and Stern 2009). In addition, in their view rape or raping was not linked to a notion of successful masculinity. A successful, celebrated man, they explained, is a man with the financial and material resources to 'keep'/'support'/'pay for' many women (Eriksson Baaz and Stern 2008). In the soldiers' testimonies, the man who rapes was, rather, an *emasculated man*, who, deprived of the resources needed to perform hegemonic masculinity, is 'forced' to rape (Eriksson Baaz and Stern 2009). Hence, in reading the soldiers' stories, 'the problem of rape' cannot be located in a simplified understanding of a violent militarised masculinity celebrating rape, nor in moral vacuums (as is often stipulated in SSR interventions in the DRC).

Lastly, let us highlight a further disparity between militarised masculinities as they were articulated in the DRC and dominant notions of what militarised masculinity entails, namely the absence of a highly gendered protector/ protected dichotomy. Military traditionalist discourses in many contexts (not the least in the US, and particularly in arguments against women's inclusion in armed forces) draw heavily on a gendered distinction between protector (men) and protected (women) (cf., Gutmann 2000; Mitchell 1989; van Creveld 2000). In this familiar gender coding, women are inherently in need of protection. In addition to being presented as a violation of natural and desired gender relations, the inclusion of women is also presented as a serious threat to combat efficiency, since military resources and energy supposedly will be used to protect the women within the army, rather than engaging with the enemy. However, while women were described as 'weak' in the DRC armed forces (therefore, not suitable for combat), they were not portrayed as eliciting, requiring or deserving special protection from men. Simply put, women were not cast as particular 'objects of protection' (Eriksson Baaz and Stern 2011).

In short, the soldiers' gendered stories of themselves demonstrate the incompleteness of the dominant imagery of a homogenised, globalised, militarised masculinity, shared by military males in military institutions worldwide. While shaped in a global landscape, military masculinities are constructed in national and local contexts (and are also often articulated in various ways in different sections and branches of the same military institution). We have addressed these processes (how specific aspects of military gendered identities in the DRC can be understood from the perspective of material, social and gender relations and norms in that country) at length in other work (Eriksson Baaz and Stern 2008, 2009, 2010, 2011) and cannot further address these issues here. Let us instead, drawing on the short overview above, highlight some weaknesses and problems in gendered SSR interventions in the DRC. What implications can be drawn from our material in terms of gender and SSR in the DRC? To what extent are current interventions aligned with the ways in which the Congolese armed forces are 'already gendered'? Clearly, there is no room for a comprehensive assessment, but let us make some broad points.

Discordant Interpretations and Interventions

First, we return to the absence of the 'protector/protected' dichotomy in the soldiers' narratives. Many observers would surely conceive of the lack of Congolese male soldiers' sense of themselves as inherent protectors of women (who, in turn, warrant such protection) as a failing that causes violence against women in the DRC, particularly rape. According to this line of reasoning, violence against women must be understood as a consequence of the failure by Congolese men to act in a way expected of 'real' honourable men and soldiers (i.e., to protect women). Educational efforts are therefore often designed to 'correct' this ignorance. Such interpretation and the consequent educative efforts, however, are deeply problematic, in that they reproduce harmful gender stereotypes, which, among other things, limit women's access to state security institutions. They are also arguably ineffective. Violence against women is a global phenomenon even in societies celebrating the man/protector, women/protected dichotomy. Sexual and gender-based violence (like all violence committed by security sector staff) must be understood in relation to myriad factors (cf., Woods 2009, 2010; Cohen 2011; Eriksson Baaz and Stern forthcoming 2012), not simply as a 'failure' to recognise the inherent victimhood of women (Eriksson Baaz and Stern 2011).

Similarly, sexual violence (or other abuse) cannot simply be explained in terms of a simplified and violent militarised masculinity that celebrates rape, nor can it be understood simply in terms of moral vacuums. In short, the main problem is not that soldiers do not understand rape to be wrong. This points to the limitations of current gender and SSR interventions, which mainly take the form of isolated workshops and training sessions for military staff.

Such workshops and training aim to educate the soldiers in human rights and international humanitarian law norms and frameworks. It is easy to see why these interventions are so tempting: they tend to be uncontroversial, are quick and easy and, in addition, provide visible proof that 'something is being done.' However, these types of information campaigns or isolated training sessions seldom have tangible effects. The main problem in most warring contexts is not that the perpetrators of rape are unaware that what they are doing is morally wrong and a crime (nor is it that women are not aware they have the right not to be raped). For effective prevention, longer-term commitments addressing structural causes of violence are needed. What these are will differ from case to case. As we have argued elsewhere (Eriksson Baaz and Stern 2010; see also Verweijen 2013 for a good analysis of potentially effective measures), in the DRC such efforts could include measures[4] such as long-term strengthening of the military justice system; addressing all forms of misconduct (rather than isolated, mobile courts focusing only on only one form of abuse); positive measures that encourage effective leadership and high professionalism among security sector staff (not simply 'reform through punishment politics');[5] efforts to improve civil-military relations by strengthening civil society's influence on the military reform process and by strengthening military commanders' willingness and capacity to engage in dialogue with local populations in their deployment areas.

By this we do not suggest we should halt efforts to 'reform' gendered military norms and identities. Surely, aspects of militarised masculinity are central to understanding the violence by the army against civilians (as in other military contexts). For instance, while rape was not celebrated by soldiers, their testimonies bear clear witness to a normalisation of sexual violence. As demonstrated above, rape appeared as normalised through the workings of the familiar myths about male heterosexuality, wherein the male soldier's libido is portrayed as a formidable natural force (and forming the basis of the notion of rape-as-substitution, common in many military institutions, see Woods 2009, 2010). Hence, aspects of militarised masculinities are certainly 'part of the problem' in the DRC as elsewhere and need to be addressed in SSR interventions.

---

4   This is in no way intended to be a comprehensive list.
5   Positive measures to foster team spirit and work pride are essential in a context where there is little satisfaction or pride and high levels of discontent and frustration linked to systematic embezzlement and fraud by military superiors. Such measures could include positive reinforcement, such as medals, providing to units that display professional behaviour income-generation activities for soldiers' families and education facilities for soldiers' children.

Our concerns are rather connected to the how question, the methods that are employed. First, it has to be recognised that norms are not only or best addressed by training or talking, but though other measures such as those identified above. One problem with the current training and workshop approach is that these events tend to be isolated, with soldiers going through a couple of days of training and then returning to their military units. Isolated events such as these will certainly not produce much change. It is only when norms-enforcement mechanisms are integrated into day-to-day military life and instruction that there will be any palpable normative and behaviour change (see Verweijen 2013 for the DRC context).

The second problem with current efforts is the underlying assumptions (the belief that soldiers are living in a moral vacuum) and that they should be cured of their ignorance and pulled out of their moral morass by being educated in international regimes on human rights. As a Congolese officer responsible for improving civil-military relations (a Civil-Military Operations officer) remarked, such attitudes are not only paternalistic (and frequently racist, we would add), ignoring the fact that soldiers 'already know' through social norms and education at home, they also fail to connect with other norm-crafting beliefs that are important to the soldiers' themselves. He explained, for instance, how he and others like him in their own efforts to address norms and change behaviour, work closely with army chaplains. References only to international human rights regimes (though they also make such references) are rather futile, according to him. Instead, discussions of masculinity, violence and ethics must also be situated within beliefs that are central to people's everyday lives. In conclusion, as we have highlighted in the in the introduction, one built-in problem in the talkshop practice of reform is the overriding import of expatriate knowledge, thereby ignoring the structural inequalities built into international SSR efforts and failing to listen to and learn from the experiences of the people concerned.

References

Cohen, D.K., 2011, *Explaining Sexual Violence During Civil War,* PhD thesis, University of Minnesota.

Enloe, C., 2000, *Maneuvers: The international politics of militarising women's lives.* Berkeley: University of California Press.

Eriksson Baaz, Maria and Maria Stern, forthcoming 2012, *Sexual Violence as a Weapon of War? Perceptions, Prescriptions, Problems in the Congo and Beyond.* London and New York: Zed Books.

Eriksson Baaz, Maria and Maria Stern, 2011, 'Whores, Men and Other Misfits: Undoing the "Feminisation" of the Armed Forces in the DR Congo,' *African Affairs* 110, issue 441 (October).

Eriksson Baaz, Maria and Maria Stern, 2010, *The Complexity of Violence: A critical analysis of sexual violence in the Democratic Republic of Congo.* Stockholm and Uppsala: Sida and the Nordic Africa Institute.

Eriksson Baaz, Maria and Maria Stern, 2009, 'Why do Soldiers Rape? Masculinity, Violence and Sexuality in the Armed Forces in the Congo,' in *International Studies Quaterly* 53:495–518.

Eriksson Baaz, Maria and Maria Stern, 2008, 'Making Sense of Violence: Voices of Soldiers in the DRC,' in *Journal of Modern African Studies* 46, no. 1.

Gutmann, Stephanie, 2000, *The Kinder, Gentler Military.* New York: Scribner's.

Higate, Paul (ed.), 2003, *Military Masculinities. Identity and the State.* Westport: Praeger.

Higate, Paul, 2004, *Gender and Peacekeeping Case Studies: The DRC and Sierra Leone,* ISS Monograph 91. Pretoria: Institute for Security Studies.

Higate, P. and J. Hopton, 2003, 'War, Militarism and Masculinities,' in Kimmel, M.S., J. Hearn and R.W. Connell (eds), *Handbook of Studies on Men and Masculinities.* Thousand Oaks CA: Sage.

Mitchell, Brian, 1998, *Women in the Military.* Washington DC: Regnery Publishing.

Mitchell, Brian, 1989, *Weak Link.* Washington DC: Regnery Publishing.

Sjoberg, L. and C.E. Gentry, 2007, *Mothers, monsters, whores: Women's violence in global politics.* London: Zed Books.

van Creveld, Martin, 2000, 'The great illusion: Women in the military,' *Millennium* 29, no. 2:429–42.

Whitworth, S., 2007, *Men, Militarism and UN Peacekeeping.* Boulder: Lynne Rienner.

Verweijen, J., 2013, 'The dialectics of protection and predation. Civilian-military interaction in Kivu, DRC,' PhD diss. in Conflict Studies, Utrecht University.

Wood, E.J., 2009, 'Armed Groups and Sexual Violence: When Is Wartime Rape Rare?,' *Politics Society* 37, no. 1:131–62.

Wood, E.J., 2010, 'Sexual Violence During War: Variation and Accountability,' in Smeulers, A. (ed.), *Collective Violence and International Criminal Justice.* Antwerp: Intersentia.

Perspectives from Both Sides
of the Thin Blue Line

Women's voices on police reform
in Liberia and Southern Sudan

Jennifer Erin Salahub

Introduction

As the concept and practice of SSR in conflict-affected developing countries
has evolved over the past decade, several challenges to its meaningful implementation have arisen. Local ownership of SSR processes, developing links to
traditional or informal justice systems[1] and integrating a gender perspective
into SSR policy and practice are all topics of recent inquiry.

However, international debates and discussions on SSR continue to focus
on traditional approaches to professionalising security sector institutions,
such as training and equipping militaries and police services, and integrating
former guerrilla fighters into statutory bodies. This focus leaves issues such
as gender, local ownership or non-statutory systems on the margins of the
debate. Moreover, the people leading and participating in such debates tend to
be male political and military elites, who often ignore the perspectives, experiences and security priorities of large populations in developing countries,
and especially marginalised groups. The perspectives of women in particular continue to be solicited infrequently and those of women in developing
countries are even more rarely heard.

Reform of police services is of particular concern to ensuring security for
the most vulnerable, due to the proximity of daily policing activities to civilian
populations. Southern Sudan and Liberia share histories of long and brutal
civil wars ending in comprehensive peace agreements, but have taken different
approaches to police reform. In Liberia, the prewar police service was vetted,
rebranded and reorganised. Gender mainstreaming and improving the gender
balance among personnel have been key priorities for the Liberia National Police (LNP). In contrast, the Southern Sudan Police Service (SSPS) was formed
following the peace agreement: it has not been vetted nor has it engendered its

---

1   See, for example, presentations made at the roundtable 'At the Margins of Security
    Sector Reform: Gender and Informal Justice,' 23 September 2010, Ottawa.

reform processes. It has consistently been a second-tier priority for the government of Southern Sudan. Both police services suffer from resource constraints. In both contexts, female police officers are a minority that is seldom heard from. And while Liberian women in civil society have been active promoters of peace and security for many years, their Southern Sudanese counterparts are much weaker. Comparing these two contexts provides a unique opportunity for learning and for drawing attention to the experiences and perspectives of women on both sides of the thin blue line.

The research presented here compares perspectives between like groups of interlocutors, rather than comparing the perspectives of respondents with a common nationality, in order to glean insights that will be relevant across cases. It shows that despite contextual differences, civil society activists in Southern Sudan and Liberia share many experiences with and perspectives on police reform in general, and gender-sensitive police reform in particular. However, the different structural antecedents and institutional approaches to integrating a gender perspective into police reform mean that Liberian and Southern Sudanese policewomen have had very different experiences and opinions on reform processes in their respective police services.[2]

The research was implemented by a multinational team of three female researchers: the Canadian author, a Sudanese academic and an independent Liberian researcher. The case study countries were chosen to enable the team to build on previous work and to compare different approaches to gender and police reform with a view to identifying lessons learned, analysing progress to date and documenting women's experiences with policing. A literature review was supplemented by key stakeholder interviews and focus group discussions with civil society activists and policewomen in Monrovia and Juba in May 2010.[3]

On the Outside: Civil Society Perspectives

In conversations with civil society activists in both countries, several points of convergence emerged, as did some key differences. Interlocutors from civil society organisations (CSOs) shared concerns about corruption, and in particular bribery, indiscipline (including drunkenness) while in uniform and a poor relationship between the community and police. Police officers working in traffic control seem to be the worst offenders, often exacting bribes from motorists. In Liberia, focus group discussion participants drew a clear line

---

2   For more detail and comprehensive results, see Salahub (2011)
3   For details on research methods, see Salahub (2011).

between this petty corruption and sexual exploitation of female civilians by male police officers. Bribes paid between men uniquely occur in cash, but 'depending on the looks,' a male police officer may request cash or sexual favours from a woman. Respondents see these as important contributing factors to the strained relationships and mistrust felt between police and community.

While their main experience with the police is as a service provider, our CSO interlocutors demonstrated considerable empathy with and insight into the situation of women in both police services. CSO respondents shared nuanced analyses of the links between the challenges faced by female police officers and the broader obstacles faced by women in Southern Sudanese and Liberian society. Issues of gender inequality – including discrimination in girls' education and early marriage – were linked to low levels of female participation in the police, and low levels of literacy and weak professional skills among female police officers. In Liberia, this analysis was extended to include longer-term promotion and career development challenges faced by policewomen.

Discrimination against female police officers was also a concern for both groups of CSOs. In both contexts, men are more often chosen for training opportunities than women. Participants' analyses of this situation identify wider societal devaluation of girls and young women (such as in education and training in preparation for policing careers) and few chances to overcome that sort of obstacle through professional development. Liberian participants were particularly attuned to this Catch 22 in light of the lowered professional standards used to bolster female recruitment. LNP officers recruited under lower standards are now at a disadvantage when it comes to promotion and professional development opportunities because they lack the necessary skills. In Southern Sudan, training and discrimination issues are linked to language patterns. Many policewomen in the SSPS speak Arabic fluently, but do not have even functional English skills. The government of Southern Sudan has chosen English as the official common language of Southern Sudan, and as a result police training is to be provided in that language. However, this means that Arabic-speaking women are not eligible to participate, further placing them at a disadvantage and perpetuating a vicious cycle. Extremely low levels of literacy across the police service exacerbate these trends.

Such training issues also directly impact civilians, sometimes disproportionately affecting those who are most vulnerable. Both Southern Sudanese and Liberian civil society activists noted that problems with training were having a negative impact on the special policing structures established to respond to sexual and gender-based violence (SGBV). Weaknesses in training and failure to implement proper protocols contribute to inappropriate and insensitive treatment of women and girls reporting SGBV. Focus group participants reported that it is not uncommon for SSPS officers to instruct a female survivor of sexual assault to deal with the issue within her family, despite the fact that her abuser may be a family member. Survivors are often re-victimised by their experience with LNP officers, who will challenge their report or ask questions such as, 'Why do you allow yourself to be raped?' Without a doubt, these are contributing factors to the low level of SGBV reporting in both contexts and to undermining the advancements made through the establishment of the Women and Children Protection Section of the LNP and the Special Protection Unit for women and children of the SSPS. As with discrimination issues, these attitudes reflect broader, entrenched social patterns.

The impact of limited resources on police service delivery and capacity concerned both CSO focus groups. Police services have limited access to vehicles and limited fuel to operate them. This is most acutely felt in rural areas, where poor infrastructure also contributes to limited service and a subsequent negative impact on both the legitimacy and public opinion of the police. Communications equipment, such as walkie-talkies, is equally limited, as are basic office supplies. Inadequate and/or unreliable payment of salaries can negatively impact police performance by creating incentives to supplement one's income through corruption. Both focus groups identified low salaries as a concern, though timely payment of salaries seems to be an issue limited to Southern Sudan.

While common experiences are useful in identifying areas for dialogue and sharing lessons learned, shedding light on divergent experiences is also important. Interlocutors in Liberia commented on a number of domestic processes and structures that do not exist in Southern Sudan, such as vetting of police personnel. Liberian CSOs consider LNP vetting to be 'incomplete' when compared with the robust vetting process for the armed forces of Liberia. In Southern Sudan, no vetting process has been initiated and there are no plans to begin one. This represents a missed opportunity to professionalise the police, many of whom were transferred from the Sudan People's Liberation Army (SPLA) without formal training and continue to have difficulty operating in a civilian environment. On the other hand, a rigorous vetting process, including educational standards, would likely decimate the SSPS and have an even greater impact on its female staff. This suggests that vetting programmes must be carefully considered in both the short and medium terms when focusing on the strategic goals of the institution in question.

Assessments of police professionalism in both countries also differ. Overall, Liberian CSOs feel that some improvements have been made, though they would welcome greater investment in priorities such as the Women and

Children Protection Service and community policing.[4] In Southern Sudan, CSO concerns about professionalism were linked to the SSPS's militarised origins, to inadequate training and professional development opportunities – including literacy and language training – and to insufficient resources. Institutionalised nepotism and tribalism in recruitment and advancement were cited as key concerns. Such a characteristic is particularly worrying for an independent South Sudan, which continues to see frequent low-level conflict along tribal lines, even if its root causes are based on issues such as resources or rites of passage. A preponderance of one tribe in a security institution should be cause for concern, considering the way in which security agencies have been instrumentalised to the benefit of one or another ethnic group in other contexts, such as Burundi. CSO participants in Southern Sudan did concede that there had been some improvements recently in community-level violence, an analysis they share with many female SSPS officers.

On the Inside: Policewomen's Perspectives

Unlike their counterparts working in CSOs, policewomen in Liberia and Southern Sudan seem to share few perspectives on their experiences with police reform. This can be largely attributed to historical and present-day contextual differences. The (re)creation of the two services has been starkly different: the LNP retrained a large number of experienced personnel from the prewar institution, whereas the SSPS was created through a transfer of second-tier ex-combatants.[5] The Liberian government has prioritised police reform while the government of Southern Sudan has placed the SSR emphasis firmly on military reform. The two institutions' approaches to integrating a gender perspective also differ significantly, with the LNP's approach being much more robust than that of the SSPS. The SSPS has some gender-sensitive policies, discussed below, but these have developed without the framework of a dedicated gender policy.

The experiences that Liberian and Southern Sudanese policewomen share reveal important practical implications for life as a female police officer – and

4   For an analysis of community policing in Liberia and Southern Sudan, see Baker (2009:372–89).
5   Interview with senior SSPS official, Juba, May 2010. See also International Crisis Group, Africa Report No. 154 (2009:19). In contrast to this characterisation, officers claimed that well-educated SPLA officers were chosen for police service. Interview with male SSPS officer and focus group discussion with policewomen, Juba, May 2010.

for developing policies on policewomen. Issues such as maternity leave, (sexual) harassment and the transfer of personnel to different duty stations around the country were raised in both focus groups. Three months' paid maternity leave is available in both locations, despite the different approaches to gender mainstreaming. In Sudan, all harassment is prohibited under the police code of conduct. In Liberia, sexual harassment within the police service and by police officers interacting with the public continues to be a challenge, despite being proscribed by a specific policy. Efforts to improve awareness of the policy and create an environment conducive to reporting have been slow to show results. Women disproportionately bear the burden of sexual harassment due to power dynamics, poor understanding of the policy and fear of professional reprisal by senior male colleagues. Transfer policies in both cases confirm that police officers cannot be transferred arbitrarily, and in Liberia the gender policy requires a policewoman's family responsibilities be taken into consideration. However, implementation of these policies is often the greatest challenge.

Divergent experiences also reveal the impact of a gender policy on awareness-raising. Southern Sudanese policewomen working without a gender policy seemed less aware of and less concerned about the gendered impact of police reform than their Liberian counterparts, who are well-versed in gender issues. (Of course, differences in education and seniority also play a role in this dynamic.) While female SSPS officers focused on challenges to the SSPS writ large, their counterparts in the LNP offered nuanced analyses of gender-sensitive policing relating to recruitment, promotion and retention of female staff members, the positive impact of women on the LNP and ways to improve gendered LNP policy and practice. When female SSPS officers did engage substantively with issues that affect men and women differently, it was often to link longstanding cultural norms to constraints on women's full participation in the police service. Southern Sudanese policewomen are well aware of discriminatory practices in education favouring boys, a bias they link to challenges in recruiting qualified female candidates into the police. Language issues are also identified as exacerbating factors that impede women's participation in training opportunities, as CSO interlocutors also lamented.

Explanations of why focus group participants joined the police also reveal useful insights that suggest avenues for policymakers to pursue in seeking to improve the gender balance in police services through recruitment and retention policies. Shared motivations included many benevolent reasons: a desire to work closely with the community and contribute to its safety and protection, or a personal quality that would contribute to improving the police. The influence of a respected person also came up in both groups. Strikingly, many

Southern Sudanese policewomen indicated that they felt the police would provide a good opportunity to spend more time with children and family, a motivation that was not shared by LNP members. This may be due to their analysis of the different demands of serving in the police versus serving in the SPLA. In Liberia, the most common response was policing as a simple means of gainful employment, though all the senior officers who gave this response went on to say that they subsequently developed 'a passion' for policing and now consider it to be much more than 'just a job.'

Lessons Learned: Enduring Challenges, Untapped Potential

The main policy-relevant lessons identified during the course of the research are:

Gender-sensitive policies or practices can be developed and implemented without a specific gender policy. Further inquiry is warranted, but the evidence suggests that a gender policy is not a necessary condition for at least some gender-sensitive policies and practices.

Strong gender policies can work quite well to mainstream gender issues throughout policing practices, as the differences between Liberia and Southern Sudan show.

Gender champions can have a profound impact. High-ranking leaders (up to and including the head of state) can significantly advance gender mainstreaming and the promotion of gender equality.

The way in which guerrilla forces are demobilised (whether formally or informally), how that demobilisation relates to SSR and the rates of female participation in those forces can profoundly affect the number and placement of women in a police service. Policymakers must be mindful that the rate of female participation does not equate with meaningful roles in the police service, particularly when it comes to qualified women in decision-making positions.

Affirmative action policies, such as lowered educational standards, often lead to positive initial results, but can have negative longer term consequences.

Discrimination in education of girls and women, low female literacy and their impact on policewomen's ability to qualify for professional development opportunities have systemic impacts on recruitment, retention and promotion of female police officers.

Holistic approaches to justice and SSR are demonstrating encouraging results on issues such as SGBV and should be strengthened.

CSOs are an untapped resource for gender-sensitive police reform. They can be useful partners that perform important context-specific training, oversight, advocacy and awareness-raising roles. They can also help foster local ownership of police reform processes and should be meaningfully consulted on a regular basis.

We also identified a number of knowledge gaps and opportunities to improve gender-sensitive police reform. Topics for future inquiry include how vulnerable groups define their security in a state-building or SSR context;[6] how women negotiate family dynamics to create space for a career in policing; the gender dynamics of corruption; how the chain of command creates opportunities and obstacles for men's and women's empowerment; what are good practices in retention of female police officers; and, the roles and potential of police spouses and professional associations of female police officers[7] in supporting police reform.

Conclusion

The work summarised in this paper is the culmination of a modest undertaking to better understand the experiences of a small group of women in two conflict-affected contexts undergoing police reform. Our data collection was not exhaustive and our results should not be considered representative of all Liberian or Southern Sudanese women's experiences. Nevertheless, the perceptions and opinions we gathered from engaged interviewees and active focus group participants provide valuable insights into women's roles in police reform, how to improve reform processes and some of the gaps in our collective understanding of gender-sensitive police reform. Further active and participatory research initiatives will help to tease out more nuances and glean greater insights into these processes, as well as create space for the voices of these important but often overlooked stakeholders.

This project has also shown the value of integrating a gender perspective into police reform processes for individual police officers, the police service as a whole and the end-users of policing services, the broader community. It has revealed both the important progress that has been made in some areas, as well as the significant room for improvement that persists in others. In Liberia, Southern Sudan and other conflict-affected contexts, many challenges remain to be addressed, not least with respect to policing and the broader sociocultural dynamics that are linked to the root causes of a number of policing-specific

---

6   This knowledge gap is also raised in Salahub and Nerland (2010).

7   The Geneva Centre for Democratic Control of Armed Forces is currently conducting a mapping study of female staff associations. The North-South Institute plans to study women's police associations in West Africa in 2011.

challenges. With the support of the international community and specifically aid donors, stakeholders in Liberia, Southern Sudan and similar contexts will be able to address the challenges and take advantage of the opportunities presented above through a more holistic approach to gender-sensitive police reform. Such an approach will allow national/territorial governments and their development partners to better realise their immediate security, stabilisation and policing goals as well as their longer term objectives regarding human development, the full realisation of women's human rights and the promotion of true gender equality.

References

Baker, B., 2009, 'A policing partnership for post-war Africa? Lessons from Liberia and southern Sudan,' *Policing and Society* 19, no. 4, 372–89.

Bastick, M., 2008, 'Integrating gender in post-conflict security sector reform,' in *SIPRI Yearbook 200.* Stockholm: SIPRI.

Bastick, M. and K. Valasek (eds), 2008, *Gender and Security Sector Reform Toolkit.* Geneva: Centre for the Democratic Control of Armed Forces (DCAF), OSCE/Office for Democratic Institutions and Human Rights and UN-International Training Institute for the Advancement of Women.

Donais, T. (ed.), 2008, *Local Ownership and Security Sector Reform.* Zurich: LIT Verlag.

International Crisis Group, 2009, *Jonglei's Tribal Conflicts: Countering Insecurity in South Sudan,* Africa Report No. 154. Brussels: International Crisis Group.

Lokuji, A.S., A.S. Abatneh and C.K. Wani, 2009, *Police Reform in Southern Sudan.* Ottawa: North-South Institute.

Mobekk, E., 2010, 'Gender, Women and Security Sector Reform,' *International Peacekeeping* 17, no. 2:278–91.

Nathan, L., 2007, *No Ownership, No Commitment: A Guide to Local Ownership of Security Sector Reform.* Birmingham: University of Birmingham.

Salahub, J.E., 2007, 'Canada, Haiti and Gender Equality in a 'Fragile State,' in *Fragile States or Failing Development? Canadian Development Report 2008*, Ottawa: North-South Institute.

Salahub, J.E. (ed.), 2011, *African Women on the Thin Blue Line: Gender-Sensitive Police Reform in Liberia and Southern Sudan.* Ottawa: North-South Institute.

Salahub, J.E. and K. Nerland, 2010, 'Just Add Gender? Challenges to Meaningful Integration of Gender in SSR Policy and Practice,' in M. Sedra (ed.), *The Future of Security Sector Reform.* Waterloo: CIGI:261–78.

Valasek, K., 2008, 'Gender and Democratic Security Governance,' in Cole, E., K. Eppert and K. Kinzelbach (eds), *Public Oversight of the Security Sector: A Handbook for Civil Society Organisatio.* Bratislava: UNDP and DCAF.

Towards a Gender-sensitive Police and Army

How the EU is assisting the DRC government reform its security apparatus

Ramadan Fabrice

Introduction

No need to tell you more about the Democratic Republic of the Congo. The facts speak for themselves because with the DRC almost everything is big, for better and worse: its size makes it the third-largest country in Africa (2,344,858 sq km); its population, 68 million people; its huge natural resources (cobalt, copper, niobium, tantalum, petroleum, industrial and gem diamonds, gold, silver, zinc, manganese, tin, uranium, coal, hydropower, timber...); the highest death toll related to conflict since the Second World War (five million dead); it is the theatre of the world's largest peacekeeping mission (MONUSCO with almost 20,000 peacekeepers); and is one of the Central African countries with a high-level of reported cases of sexual violence.[1]

Against the backdrop of this post-conflict situation, the EU has deployed two security sector reform missions: EUSEC RD CONGO (since 2005) to assist the Congolese government reform its army, the FARDC (Force Armées de la République Démocratique du Congo); and EUPOL RD CONGO (since 2007), the sister mission involved in reforming the police, the PNC (Police Nationale Congolaise). The main objective of those two CSDP (Common Security and Defence Policy) missions is contributing to the formation of a well-trained, well-managed and strong police and army, able to secure the borders of the vast country and maintain public order while respecting human rights and fundamental freedoms. An emphasis has been put on gender, especially the fight against sexual violence too often committed by men in uniform.

Different tools are being used to have a gender-sensitive army and police in the DRC: from promoting more women in uniform to setting up structures to prevent and repress gender-based violence committed by uniformed men. Gender and gender equality are recognised in the country not only through

---

1   UN Population Fund statistics reported 17,507 cases of sexual violence in 2009 for the entire country and 2,243 in the first half of 2010 for North Kivu province alone.

the laws and the constitution, but also by all the missions and NGOs working in the DRC, many of which have a gender component. Unfortunately, the progress being made is reversible because of the ongoing conflict (especially in the Kivus in the eastern part of the country), the fragile political will and the extreme poverty. SSR in a poor country is quite different from that in a rich and developed one.

Promotion of Women Within the Congolese Security Forces

There's a legal obligation on the Congolese government to eliminate all forms of discrimination against women and to promote their fair representation within national institutions. This is enshrined in Article 14 of the 2006 constitution of the country. There is also a draft bill on the implementation of gender parity, including a quota policy for more women in different institutions, including the army and police. But this legal achievement is not yet a reality.

As a result of EUSEC RD CONGO's support for two biometrical censuses conducted in 2008 and in 2009, we know approximately the total number of men and women serving in the armed forces. There are now 150,000 military. Before the last census and according to statistics given by the Congolese ministry of defence, there were more than 3,456 female soldiers out of a total of 129,407, or only 3 per cent.

So many prejudices exist about a female soldier: she's a prostitute, a person unsuccessful in her life, someone who got her position because she was good at nothing. Within the army, some are viewed as 'meat for the superior,' ready to obey and satisfy any sexual desire of the commanders. The reality is the same for the police, even if today there are no credible figures on the number of men and women serving in the Congolese police. But the PPF[2] or policewoman feels just as discriminated against as the PMF[3] or female soldier.

During a roundtable organised by EUSEC, EUPOL and REJUSCO[4] in March 2010 in Goma[5] in order to celebrate 'International Woman's Day,' one female army captain downplayed the discrimination and preferred to put the blame on the PMFs because of their lack of character or education. This attitude was a great challenge in my work as gender advisor. Every time I tried to recruit female soldiers or policewomen for EUSEC and EUPOL training

2   Personnel Policier Féminin.
3   Personnel Militaire Féminin.
4   REJUSCO (Restauration de la Justice à l'Est du Congo) was a justice reform programme funded by the EU Commission, DFID and other European countries.
5   Goma is in the eastern part of the DRC.

and other activities, I struggled to find educated and assertive women. Many of those in Goma speak no French or never went to school. Some explain this situation by the fact that some of these women joined the security forces not through traditional channels but through personal ones. As long as this situation continues, we will have the same results.

In the ongoing process of the army and police reform in the DRC, there need to be some incentives in order to increase female participation. These should include:

a. Strict and unbiased criteria for joining the army and police. Women should be recruited based on their abilities and not on their personal ties with commanders;

b. Good pay, social benefits, leave, medical care, housing, so that recruits can earn a decent living as a policewoman or female soldier (the average pay for a soldier or policeman is now $50, which is insufficient);

c. Strict and unbiased criteria for promotion (e.g., no need to have personal ties with someone to get promotion).

I believe women can make a difference within the security forces if they have the necessary qualifications, education and personality to play their roles in uniform

Fight Against Gender-Based Violence by the Security Forces

When it comes to gender-based violence, the accusatory finger first points at the men in uniform in the DRC. Gender-based violence is multifaceted: it includes sexual violence, forced marriage, domestic violence or spouse abuse.

There are many legal instruments addressing gender-based violence in the DRC:

a. Article 15 of the Congolese constitution mentions the fight against sexual violence and Article 45 mentions the state's obligation to integrate human rights courses (implicitly gender courses) in the training of security forces;

b. The Sexual Violence Act (2006) and Child Protection Act (2009);

c. The National Strategy on Gender-based Violence in the DRC;[6]

d. The Comprehensive Strategy on Combating Sexual Violence;[7]

---

6 This document is the Congolese government's strategy to fight gender-based violence

7 This document creates a coordination mechanism for national and international partners working on the issue of sexual violence. It includes five working groups.

Over the last 10 years, women and young girls have been particularly targeted during the conflict. Rape was used as a weapon of war by all the parties. Today, things are changing. Rape as a weapon of war is less and less the reality (in spite of the Walikalé ordeal when almost 300 persons, including men, were raped from 30 July to 2 August 2010).[8] More and more rape is now perpetrated by civilians. However, this is no excuse for inaction.[9]

That is why EUSEC and EUPOL are assisting the Congolese security forces in preventing and repressing gender-based violence by men in uniform through various measures, particularly:

a. A clean criminal record before recruitment. If this draft bill is passed, perpetrators of sexual violence will be prevented from joining the security forces;

b. Adoption of a *code of good conduct for the army and a projected code of ethics* for the police as a reminder of their obligation not to harm the population;

c. Setting up an internal structure to oversee respect for human rights and codes of ethics (Inspection Générale D'Audit or IGA for the police and conseil de discipline for the army). EUPOL helped train the IGA inspectors, whose mandate includes investigating cases of human rights violation by the police;

d. Rehabilitating the army training school: The DRC is one of the few countries in Africa not to have regular training schools for privates, non-commissioned officers or officers. To fill that vacuum, many external partners, including EUSEC and EUPOL, are training the security forces 'à la carte' on gender and sexual violence;

e. Standardising the police training module, especially on combating sexual violence. This activity is being undertaken through the CSRP (Comité de Suivi de le Réforme de la Police), which designs police reform along with nine working groups, including a sexual violence, human rights and child protection working group, in which EUPOL experts play a critical role;

f. Training soldiers and policemen on how to fight sexual violence and training in 'proximity policing,' which includes the recommendation to have more qualified policewomen to welcome and interview victims of sexual violence;

g. Setting-up well-equipped and well-trained sexual-violence units in police

---

8 The Office of High Commissioner for Human Rights has released a preliminary report on the mass rapes in Walikalé.

9 According to UN Population Fund statistics for the first half of 2010, 49 per cent of the perpetrators in the 2,243 reported cases of sexual violence are civilians.

stations. One such PSPE-F (Police Spéciale de la Protection de l'Enfant et de la Femme) unit exists in Goma in a new office built with GTZ (German cooperation) funding;

h. Sensitisation of security forces to eliminate bad practices by men in uniform, such as the rape of young girls or Pygmies in order to be rendered invulnerable in combat; and

i. Revitalisation of the FARDC internal sensitisation structure *(Service d'Education Civique et Patriotique)*, whose mission includes distributing the code of good conduct and educating soldiers on various issues, including sexual violence.

Women In Uniform and Sexual Violence
How can they Prevent Sexual Violence Being Committed by Men in Uniform?

Ultimately, the real question is will the presence of more women in the security forces prevent or reduce the level or sexual violence by men in uniform in the DRC?

The answer is not so simple and depends on many parameters. First, in my job in the DRC I tried as hard as possible to get information about sexual violence committed by men in uniform, including the profile of the perpetrators, the victims and especially the crime scene.

The last piece of information is important, because it may help the army and police develop preventive solutions, including *gendered solutions*. So, in what contexts did sexual violence take place?

1. During military operations
2. In custody
3. On night patrols
4. In a military or police camp

For military operations, the presence of more women is no guarantee of less sexual violence unless the women have command or are leading the operations. But this will require that they have a strong personality so that they have the respect of their male colleagues. In custody, the presence of more women may help reduce sexual violence committed by policemen on female suspects. Here, gender can strengthen operational effectiveness by having a woman present to arrest, search and put in custody other women. If possible, women should even be on duty at night. For night patrols, of course mixed patrols with men and women in uniform can be reassuring for women walking at night. The presence of women in uniform may prevent their male colleagues from commiting sexual abuse during such patrols. In military and police camps, the presence of more women is not the absolute solution to sexual violence, because these contain living areas and sometimes sexual violence is part of spousal abuse.

So, more women in the army or police could prevent sexual violence by men in uniform but this solution is not enough. It needs to be complemented by:

1. A functional and effective justice system (punishment is one of the best sources of prevention);
2. Good training for the security forces;
3. Vetting before recruitment;
4. Decent work conditions (pay, housing, social benefits).

Challenges and Pitfalls in Gendering the Congolese Security Forces

There are many serious obstacles to making the Congolese security forces more gender-sensitive:

Persistence of war

The army is involved in ongoing military operations. In 2010, more than one-third of the force was thus involved. Thanks to UNHCR and its cluster protection activity,[10] regular reports on human rights violations are published and many of the perpetrators are men in uniform. These violations include sexual violence.

Persistence of the 'integration process'

Over the last five years, there has been almost no normal recruitment process for the security forces, especially in the east of the country. Ex-combatants leaving the bush are integrated into the security forces in the name of peace. Sometimes, the integration takes place without vetting and appropriate training. Anyone who has committed serious crimes, including sexual violence, was able to join the security forces without fear of prosecution.

This is why I distinguish between legal recruitment, which I consider the 'choice of peace,' and integration, which I call the 'price of peace.' In the first

---

10 Clusters are forums where many actors, national and international, working on humanitarian and security meet on regular basis.

instance, you choose who will be part of the security force (implicitly, after training and a vetting) and in the latter you do not.

Persistence of impunity

Many men in uniform are still immune from prosecution. Even when they are accused of serious crimes, the military justice system is unable or unwilling to prosecute them, sometimes in the name of peace. The most notorious case is Bosco Ntganda, a general of the Congolese army but wanted by the International Criminal Court for war crimes and crimes against humanity.

The job of a military prosecutor or *auditeur militaire* is not easy in the DRC, especially in the Kivus. Either the work is hindered by the military command (a prosecutor needs, for instance, authorisation of the commandant of the region, the highest ranking position in a province, to arrest or interrogate a military officer) or by lack of resources.

But last year, the government launched a 'zero tolerance' operation aiming at ending the vicious cycle of impunity within the Congolese army and police. Many trials were held by the military justice system against uniformed men suspected of serious crimes, including sexual violence. Even if there was no balance sheet for these trials (how many men in uniform were prosecuted and judged, their rank, the crimes committed) and no monitoring of adherence to international standards, the government wanted to show its political will to fight impunity.

Low pay

Earning around $50 per month and being permanently armed with machine-gun is no excuse for committing abuses, but can be conducive to misconduct. Some soldiers try to exonerate themselves and blame their low salaries for their inability to marry a woman or to visit a prostitute.

Low salaries are also an obstacle to attracting more women into the security forces. One female soldier told me that if she worked for me as a housekeeper, she would earn maybe four times her salary as an officer in the Congolese army.

Another consequence of the lack of appropriate resources for the army and police is the persistent lack of equipment, especially food supplies for troops on operations or for the deployment of the police. Instead of providing security to the population, the security forces are more often a source of insecurity due to their so-called abandonment by the government. They have to live off the local population in many ways, including satisfying their sexual needs.

High illiteracy among women and young girls

One of the striking forms of discrimination against women and young girls is illiteracy. This sad reality is unfortunately present within the security forces. To have more capable and assertive women serving in the defence forces, the DRC needs to put more resources into the education of young girls.

In the garrison of Goma for instance, there are less than 100 PMFs. Only a few of them went to school and can actually read and write. So, to organise training for the army or to have women in uniform present for the round-table on women and SSR, it was hard to find an educated female soldier. This is a sad reality I dealt with everyday.

During the celebration of International Literacy Day on 8 September this year, with the theme the 'Power of Women's Literacy,' UNESCO released the figures for the DRC: there are 18 million illiterate people in the country and women and young girls unfortunately represent the majority.

Conclusion

Is it possible to promote gender in SSR in a post-conflict country? The answer is yes. But it is difficult because of the many obstacles such as lack of resources, fragile political will, high illiteracy among women and girls and some persistent backward-looking traditions.

But let's not be naïve: promoting gender in a country like the DRC also means respecting its culture and traditions. Having more women in the armed forces comes with a pricetag that needs to be paid: education and qualifications. Women with education, qualifications and some personality can make a difference in the security forces.

In the end, it all comes down to one thing: the world can be more proactive about gendering security forces but nothing replaces the determination of national governments. That's what the EU is trying to do with EUSEC and EUPOL: help the Congolese government take ownership of this enterprise. The task is difficult, but not impossible.

References

Office of High Commissioner for Human Rights, 2011, 'A Preliminary Report of the Mass Rapes in Walikalé, DRC,' *2010 Country Reports on Human Rights Practices,* US Bureau of Democracy, Human Rights, and Labor, US Department of State.

United Nations Population Fund (UNFPA), 2010, *The State of World Population 2010,* UNFPA.

Young Women in African Wars*

Chris Coulter, Mariam Persson and Mats Utas

Introduction

The focus on women and girls who actively participate in armed conflicts in Africa has increased significantly in recent decades. Yet despite extensive research and documentation, in mainstream studies and in most policy programming they are largely absent. Female fighters, if they appear at all, are often seen as an anomaly and child soldiers are often equated with boys. When women and girls are mentioned, it is often implied they are predominantly civilians and thus predominantly 'victims,' while male fighters are uniformly described as 'combatants' or alternatively 'perpetrators.' In reality, both male and female fighters function in a variety of roles. Women, alongside men, kill soldiers and civilians, carry out atrocities, destroy property and participate in looting for the purpose of personal enrichment. Women may participate in a number of ways, as spies, as commanders, or in logistical support roles. However, it is evident that most women and girls are also victims of war: girls and women are sexually abused, forced to work and to take up arms. The experiences of girls and women in fighting forces are thus multifaceted and complex, in that they may be both victims and perpetrators. Therefore, it is our contention that a too narrow focus on women as only victims rarely helps to 'empower' them in conflict zones and may even make it difficult to identify their real needs and thus to create emergency and development aid that works 'on the ground.'

Women and War

Even today in most analyses of war and violent conflict, women and men are often positioned at opposite ends of a moral continuum, with women generally considered peaceful and men aggressive, women passive and men active, women victims and men perpetrators. In this perspective, war remains an exclusively male concern, and women are only seen as victims and are therefore denied agency. Unlike men, they are not perceived as actors in social, economic and political structures. Therefore, viewing women as more nurtu-

---

* This text was first published as a NAI Policy Note in 2007.

ring and peaceful both supports and reproduces patriarchal values in war as well as peace. Quite often, many men and women do assume these roles, but the reality is that women are also active as fighters, while men may well also be victims. In mainstream literature, there has been a tendency to exaggerate the extent to which men and women play stereotypical gender roles in armed conflict.

Victims or perpetrators?

If women stereotypically are regarded as more peaceful, what then do people think of women as soldiers/fighters/rebels? In many wars and violent conflicts, for example Rwanda, Sierra Leone, Mozambique, Uganda and Eritrea, women have shown themselves to be as capable as men of performing violent acts. However, as soldiering has been included in the moral universe of men in ways that it has not for women, fighting women are frequently considered to be transgressing accepted female behaviour, and the very act of fighting by definition makes women and girls less feminine and by extension 'unnatural' or 'deviant.' Despite the increasing number of women in armed groups, 'the soldier' is still conceived of as a man. The presence of female fighters thus both disturbs and complicates conventional notions of war.

Overview of Young Women in Armed Conflicts in Africa

It is believed that women and girls participate in armed conflicts in Africa to a far greater degree than has previously been recognised. Women have been actively involved as fighters in African countries as diverse as Angola, Eritrea, Ethiopia, Liberia, Mozambique, Sierra Leone, South Africa, Uganda and Zimbabwe. Some of these were wars of liberation from colonial powers, while others are current rebel insurgencies, and in these conflicts women have served in a range of capacities, from foot soldiers to high-ranking positions. Today, young women in Africa participate in insurgencies and rebel movements, but they are also frequently employed in state-sanctioned violence.

Abduction or voluntary conscription?

The mode of conscription of girls and women into armed forces varies, just as it does for boys and men. Some are abducted and forcefully conscripted, while others join for ideological reasons or as a survival strategy. The distinction between the various forms is also complex. Although the abduction and forced conscription of women and girls is commonplace, recent research has shown that some feel there are beneficial aspects to joining.

Status, positions and roles of young women in war

The status positions of female fighters vary from conflict to conflict and between different fighting forces. It is important to note that African women's experience as fighters is not uniform and varies considerably by local context. Within patriarchal societies, such as Mozambique, Uganda and Sierra Leone, where women and girls are oppressed in countless ways, this oppression often seems also to be reflected in the structure of the fighting forces. In these, women and girls carry out traditional gender roles such as cooking, cleaning and serving men, seemingly replicating the tasks they perform in society at large. However, it has also been noted that women's and girls' participation in fighting forces can bring about new opportunities for them, such as achieving positions of power and learning skills previously out of reach. War can thus oppress women and girls while at the same time expanding their opportunities.

Female fighters may gain status and control, and feel pride, self-confidence and a sense of belonging by bearing arms. However, as has also been noted, except for the most powerful female fighters who have commander status or are important 'wives' of high commanders, most female fighters are also subjected to abuse by men and boys due to their low position in the gender hierarchy.

Sex slaves or labour force?

Many of the young women that have been abducted or forcefully conscripted have also been exposed to sexual violence. But was this the principal reason for their abduction? We argue that one important aspect has received too little attention in most writing on abduction and conscription in many African wars: women's productive labour.

Even during war, the chores of everyday life have to be performed – cooking, cleaning and doing laundry. Women in armed insurgencies in Africa are also involved in trading and trafficking looted goods, and in agricultural production. The roles young women perform in armed insurgency groups in Africa go far beyond being simple 'sex slaves' or 'camp followers.' Rather, they are essential to the functioning and maintenance of the war system itself. Rebel movements in Africa often need women and children to maintain this system and abduct them for that reason.

However, it seems clear from the conflicts in Africa in recent decades that rapes and sexual violence against young women, female fighters included, are widespread. Therefore, any analysis of female fighters in Africa has to inquire into this issue, and more importantly be sensitive to and contribute to an understanding of local concepts of rape or sexual stigma in order to help address these issues on the ground.

Female Fighters: Disarmament and Demobilisation

The frameworks for most DDR programmes for combatants are set and negotiated in official peace agreements. The aims of the projects are basically (1) to collect, register and destroy all conventional weapons; (2) to demobilise combatants; and (3) to reintegrate ex-combatants. Those combatants who are enrolled in DDR programmes are usually provided with some monetary and material assistance and are also frequently given weeks or months of vocational or literacy training. As we have described above, there are a considerable number of female fighters in various fighting forces in Africa, although no one knows exactly how many. Most agree, however, that those women and girls who have registered in DDR programmes in Africa are very few and do not accurately represent the real number of female fighters. In most DDR processes in African countries with high numbers of women in fighting forces, there is a low turnout of girls and women because, it is assumed, most women do not demobilise unless specific measures are made to include them in the process.

Female fighters excluded from DDR programmes

The reason for not working actively to include girls and women in institutionalised DDR programmes could be that female fighters also perform additional roles – they are labourers, 'wives,' girlfriends, domestic workers, farmers – and this can render the notion of who is a fighter and who is not unclear. They are frequently misrepresented as only dependants or wives of male fighters, and as 'camp followers,' and few efforts are made to determine whether they in fact were also fighters. Their different roles may prevent the UN, aid organisations and ordinary civilians from seeing girls and women as 'real' fighters, thereby screening them out of the process of demobilisation. As discussed above, we argue that those women who are only thought of as abducted women or sex slaves, and who as such are excluded from formal demobilisation, have actually formed the backbone of many armed forces, and have been vital to the war enterprise.

Lately, there have been attempts to broaden the definition of combatant.

However, although both UN Resolution 1325 and the Cape Town Principles address this issue and include in the category of combatant not only those carrying guns, this has not improved the situation of female fighters, who continue to be excluded from DDR efforts. Therefore, if the intention is to reach all fighters, it is essential to understand the mechanisms behind female fighters' lack of access to official DDR programmes and why they sometimes choose not to participate.

Avoiding DDR

Many female ex-fighters may choose not to take part in official DDR programmes out of fear or the feeling that they have nothing to gain but much to lose by attending. This can be a question of security in the demobilisation camps, as has been attested by fighters in Sierra Leone. The facilities were perceived to be dangerous for women and girls, because of the large numbers of men and inadequate protection. Special safe, secure and single-sex centres for the demobilisation of women with predominantly female staff should therefore be provided.

Female ex-fighters may also not turn up for disarmament and demobilisation for fear of having their identities as former fighters revealed. This is a very central aspect that we argue has not been seriously dealt with in the planning and implementation of DDR programmes. There is often a considerable stigma attached to female fighters, and women and girls may feel that registering at the DDR centres and joining the programmes will only result in further social exclusion by the civil community. Given that female fighters are not easily accepted back into civil society and often looked upon with fear and suspicion, there is a real risk that these apprehensions may be justified. The negative attitudes that civilian societies often have towards female ex-fighters, as well as the issue of shame and the threat of stigmatisation of these women and girls, must be seriously considered when DDR processes are planned. The challenge is to reach female ex-fighters without simultaneously contributing to their stigmatisation. Such assistance must recognise as its point of departure that female ex-fighters may lack social networks due to rejection by families and male partners.

Surviving War - Surviving Peace: Post-conflict Challenges

Female ex-combatants are by definition those that survived war. Over years in the fighting forces, often under immense pressure, these women and girls learned survival techniques and made tactical choices, and they acquired skills and strengths that kept them alive. But surviving war does not automatically make peace an easy project. While the roles and status positions of female combatants vary widely during war, what most of them seem to share is limited access to benefits at the time of peace and demobilisation.

Changing gender roles?

War often entails a temporary change in gender roles. Even though it may not be true for all women and girls, life as a female fighter can bring about opportunities to achieve positions of power and gain agency in a way not possible prior to the war. In some cases, women manage to change their status positions after war too, but frequently they revert to more traditional or conservative gender roles. When male and female ex-fighters return to civil society, they are often received differently. While men are perceived to have strengthened their gender role through life in the fighting forces, women are instead increasingly marginalised. During and after the Mozambican war of liberation, for example, new female roles emerged, urged and supported by FRELIMO. However, after the war FRELIMO either failed to provide support for or directly opposed the gender struggle of women.

Opportunities to support gender equality in many post-conflict situations have often not been seized. Traditional gender stereotypes and divisions of labour have instead often been reintroduced, and sometimes even reinforced by DDR programmes. Post-conflict settings can bring about opportunities with regard to equality between women and men and the expansion of traditional gender norms. However, such changes do not come easily. It has to be acknowledged that although war can oppress women and girls in countless ways, it may expand their opportunities and contribute to gender equality. It is of fundamental importance that these opportunities are acknowledged.

Skills and strengths

Despite traumatic war experiences and life under immense pressure, female ex-fighters are among those who have survived war. However, it is evident that the skills and strengths female fighters acquired during their time in fighting forces will never be acknowledged if women continue to be regarded as passive victims. By treating them as such or or as 'dependants,' and by not acknowledging the skills and resources they have acquired, female ex-fighters are again stripped of control of their lives and a sense of dignity. DDR programmes thereby also risk squandering tremendous social capital that could be of importance to post-conflict reconstruction.

Shame and stigma

Stigmatisation is often a reality for many former female fighters. Upon returning to civil society, these women and girls are often looked upon with suspicion and fear as perpetrators of violence and for violating established gender roles. In Sierra Leone, many female ex-fighters said that they had been so badly treated and disliked by civilians they became ashamed of having stayed so long with the fighting forces. The feelings of shame often originated from being called a rebel or having a 'rebel child.' One effect of the social stigma is that many women and girls hide their past and do not come forward to receive the DDR-benefits they are entitled to. Another consequence is the difficulty of getting married. This is of great importance in many African societies, as marriage is seen as mandatory for women. Unmarried women are sometimes likened to social outcasts. In cultures where women's access to land, property, social networks and status is determined to a large extent by her husband and his clan, a woman's inability to marry poses serious challenges to her human security and livelihood options.

Education

Many female ex-fighters express a strong wish to gain access to education for themselves and their children once the war is over. According to some, this wish is especially expressed by young women who had been abducted or pressured into armed forces, had been held as forced wives or had given birth to children as a result of these unwanted relationships. Related to this is the fact that young mothers are often among those most stigmatised. These young women probably see education as an opportunity to regain control of their lives and to offer their children a future.

Health

Most female ex-fighters return from war with physical and psychological health problems. The suffering from problems such as STDs, often due to sexual violence and abuse, contributes to the overall psychological effects of war traumas that female ex-fighters also experience. In addition, such health problems may cause further stigmatisation in civil society, leaving these young women even more vulnerable. Testing, treating and educating female ex-fighters in relation to STDs and other diseases and health problems should therefore be complemented by psychological assistance and counselling, if the young women so wish.

Livelihood options

While many NGOs emphasise that their objective in postwar societies is to make women independent and self-reliant, few ask if the skills they offer lead to sustainable livelihoods. In creating livelihood options for young female ex-fighters, it is essential to examine their social position and the links between being able to make a living and social well-being, between economy and social life: the sociocultural background is of the utmost importance in planning postwar rehabilitation projects. One issue seldom addressed by organisations targeting abducted and ex-combatant women is that their ability to reintegrate into postwar society is not only a question of their generating an income but also largely of how they are viewed in postwar society. It matters little how many projects a female ex-combatant participates in if her ability to put her skills into practice is circumscribed by society's negative view of her. For these and other reasons, many female ex-combatants do not always view NGO projects as their best option. Some choose other ways to survive. And those who have only their bodies to trade become 'girlfriends' or prostitutes. The fact that postwar prostitution often involves women who have been subject to wartime rape also speaks to the continuation of structural violence. Unfortunately, prostitution as a postwar survival strategy is quite common, and in war-torn countries with large resident peacekeeping or humanitarian aid interests, this prostitution is often described and acknowledged for what it is, a survival strategy.

Conclusion

The experiences of women and girls in fighting forces are multifaceted and complex and such females may simultaneously be victims and perpetrators. To fully comprehend what women really do in war-torn societies, it must be acknowledged that women not only have their own agenda but also that 'women' as a social category is highly differentiated. Women can be active participants in war, supporters and advocates of continued armed struggle. They can be spies, soldiers, rebels, but still – and this is an important distinction to make – women's choices in times of conflict and war are often circumscribed in ways that men's are not.

References

Barth, Elise F., 2002, *Peace as Disappointment: The Reintegration of Female Soldiers in Post-Conflict Societies, a Comparative Study from Africa*. Oslo: International Peace Research Institute (PRIO).

Coulter, Chris, 2009, *Bush Wives and Girl Soldiers: Women's lives through war and peace in Sierra Leone*. Ithaca: Cornell University Press.

Mazurana, Dyan, 2005, *Women in Armed Opposition Groups in Africa and the Promotion of International Humanitarian Law and Human Rights*. Geneva: PSIO.

Mazurana, Dyan and Christopher Carlson, 2004, *From Combat to Community: Women and Girls of Sierra Leone*. Washington DC: Women Waging Peace Policy Commission.

McKay, Susan and Dyan Mazurana, 2004, *Where Are the Girls? Girls in Fighting Forces in Northern Uganda, Sierra Leone and Mozambique: Their Lives During and After War*. Quebec: Rights and Democracy.

Notes on Contributors

Maria Eriksson Baaz is an associate professor at the School of Global Studies, University of Gothenburg and a senior researcher at the Nordic Africa Institute, Uppsala. Her research interests are in African politics, security and development, postcolonial theory and gender. Recently, she has focused on masculinity, militarisation and defence reform interventions, with a particular emphasis on the Democratic Republic of Congo. She is the co-author (with Maria Stern) of *Sexual Violence as a Weapon of War? Perceptions, Prescriptions, Problems in the Congo and Beyond* (London: Zed, 2013) and the author of *The Paternalism of Partnership: A Postcolonial Reading of Identity in Development Aid* (London: Zed 2005). She has also contributed to several policy reports such as 'The Complexity of Violence: A Critical Analysis of Sexual Violence in the Democratic Republic of Congo (DRC)' with Maria Stern (Sida and the Nordic Africa Institute, 2010).

Chris Coulter works as a senior consultant at Indevelop and holds a PhD in Social Anthropology from Uppsala University. Her research focuses on gender, conflict and post-conflict, sociocultural analysis, strategy and methodology development. She is the author of *Bush Wives and Girl Soldiers: Women's lives through war and peace in Sierra Leone* (Ithaca NY: Cornell University Press, 2009).

Cheryl Hendricks is a senior research fellow at the Conflict Management and Peacebuilding Division of the Institute for Security Studies, Pretoria. She holds a PhD from the University of South Carolina in Government and International Relations and an MA in Southern African Studies from the University of York in England. Prior to her ISS appointment, she worked as a policy analyst at the Institute for Justice and Reconciliation, an academic manager for the Centre for Conflict Resolution and as a lecturer in Political Studies at the University of the Western Cape. She has worked extensively on the issue of gender and security sector reform.

Paul Higate is reader in Gender and Security in the School for Sociology, Politics and International Studies at the University of Bristol. He has written on military masculinities in the armed forces, peacekeeping operations and, most recently, private military and security companies. He is editor of *Military Masculinities: Identity and the State* (Westport CT: Praeger, 2003) and author of numerous articles and book chapters.

Kathleen Jennings is a researcher at the Fafo Institute for Applied International Studies in Oslo. Her research focuses on UN peacekeeping, gender and security issues.

Fabrice Mickaël Ramadan Mamata is a gender expert graduate in Diplomacy and Negotiations. He has more than five years of experience in the fields of gender and human rights. Currently, he is working for the UN in Central Africa as a Lord's Resistance Army focal-point. The LRC is a Ugandan rebel movement responsible for gender-based atrocities and crimes such as sexual slavery, sexual violence and the abduction of children. Prior to that, he worked for the European Commission on an assessment of the Democratic Republic of Congo's national strategy against gender-based violence and on a peace and security project in Nigeria and Côte d'Ivoire. He also worked for 18 months as a gender advisor for the: EUPOL (police reform) and EUSEC (army reform) missions.

Mariam Persson is a PhD candidate at the Department of War Studies, King's College, London and a research assistant at the Swedish National Defence College. Her current research is focused on ex-combatants and informal security provision in Liberia. In addition, she has conducted fieldwork in Sierra Leone and the Central African Republic and has published on areas such as informal security provision in relation to security sector reform in Liberia, and female combatants in African wars.

Jennifer Erin Salahub is a senior researcher and team leader in the North-South Institute's Fragile and Conflict-Affected States programme. Her research interests focus on the nexus between security and development, security sector reform and the gender dimensions of conflict, peacebuilding and state fragility. Her recent publications include *African Women on the Thin Blue Line: Gender-Sensitive Police Reform in Liberia and Southern Sudan* (editor) (Ottawa: North-South Institute, 2011) and (with Stephen Baranyi), 'Police reform and democratic development in lower-profile fragile states' (*Canadian Journal of Development Studies*, Vol. 32, No. 1, 2011). Ms. Salahub's MA in Political Science is from McGill University and her BA in International Relations is from the University of British Columbia.

Maria Stern is a professor in Peace and Development Studies at the School of Global Studies, University of Gothenburg. Her research interests are in security studies, the security-development nexus, the politics of identity and feminist theory. Recently she has focused on masculinity, militarisation and defence reform interventions, with a particular focus on the Democratic Republic of Congo. She is the co-author (with Maria Eriksson Baaz) of *Sexual Violence as a Weapon of War? Perceptions, Prescriptions, Problems in the Congo and Beyond* (London: Zed, 2013), co-editor of *Feminist Methodologies for International Relations* (Cambridge: Cambridge University Press, 2006) and author of *Naming Security, Constructing Identity* (Manchester: Manchester University Press, 2005). She has also contributed to several policy reports, such as 'The Complexity of Violence: A Critical Analysis of Sexual Violence in the Democratic Republic of Congo (DRC)' with Maria Eriksson Baaz (Sida and Nordic Africa Institute, 2010).

Mats Utas is an associate professor in Cultural Anthropology and leader of the *Conflict, Security and Democratic Transformation Cluster* at the Nordic Africa Institute. He has written extensively on child and youth combatants, the politics and economy of informality, contested sovereignties, media, refugees and gender in conflict and war zones. He has also researched street life, informality and alternative forms of organisation in urban centres. Utas has conducted fieldwork in Liberia, Sierra Leone, Côte d'Ivoire and Somalia. He is the editor of *African conflicts and informal power: Big Men and Networks* (London: Zed, 2012), the co-editor (with Henrik Vigh and Catrine Christiansen) of *Navigating youth, generating adulthood: Social becoming in an African context* (Uppsala: Nordic Africa Institute, 2006) and the author of numerous journal articles and book chapters.